WE-hood

WE-hood

in
Human Dialogue and the Divine

RALPH M. REEVES, MD
Foreword by Gregory Alan Stoddard

RESOURCE *Publications* • Eugene, Oregon

WE-HOOD
in Human Dialogue and the Divine

Copyright © 2020 Ralph M. Reeves. All rights reserved. Except for brief quotations in critical publications or reviews, no part of this book may be reproduced in any manner without prior written permission from the publisher. Write: Permissions, Wipf and Stock Publishers, 199 W. 8th Ave., Suite 3, Eugene, OR 97401.

Biblical quotations are from either the King James Version, or the Revised Standard Version, as indicated.

Revised Standard Version, Old Testament section copyright 1952, by the Division of Christian Education of the National Council of Churches of Christ in the United States of America.

New Testament section copyright 1964 by the Division of Christian Education of the National Council of Churches of Christ in the United States of America.

Evangelical Lutheran Worship (*ELW*), copyright 2006 by Augsburg FortressResource Publications.

An Imprint of Wipf and Stock Publishers
199 W. 8th Ave., Suite 3
Eugene, OR 97401

www.wipfandstock.com

PAPERBACK ISBN: 978-1-7252-5164-9
HARDCOVER ISBN: 978-1-7252-5165-6
EBOOK ISBN: 978-1-7252-5166-3

Manufactured in the U.S.A.   04/17/20

to God the Trinity,
and to all my patients, family, and friends
who have been with me
through my slow learning

Contents

Foreword by Gregory Alan Stoddard	ix
Chapter 1: Celebrating Relationships	3
Using actual quotes	4
The field: mystery, presence, and openness	7
Your choices	8
Chapter 2: Meeting the Co-creators	10
Diane	10
Broader realms for Diane's co-statement	13
Failures at co-creation	14
Diane's life functions: fruit and seed	16
Focusing on Carol and her history	18
Unification and spirit: How might science simulate this?	20
The power of words	20
Emily: "So I won't have to lie"	21
Frances on giving herself	23
Talking about our relationship itself: Johnny, Roland, and Thomas	24
Chapter 3: General Properties of Co-created Statements	28
Artificially constructed co-statements	29
The co-statement: both mutuality and challenge	30
Chapter 4: Co-dialogue: How Does It Work?	31
The scientific/descriptive method	35
Chapter 5: On Relationship Itself	42
"The Quickening"	44

Contents

    Dimensions of Relationship   45
    Contents of mutuality: window and mirror   45
    Counter-examples   49
    The nitty-gritty of relationship energy   52
    The tendency to repair the field   54
    New levels of mental ability; new types of relationship   54

Chapter 6: "Tum Tose" Points Toward the Trinity   57
    "Tum Tose"   58

Chapter 7: Benefiting with Each Other in the Image of God as Trinity   62
    Expanding our Understandings of Relationship   62
    The image of God in Individuals and in Relationships   64
    The Trinity is a paradox: both cosmic and particular   64
    Parallels of WE-ness between divine and human   68
    Welcoming the Trinity   70
    The uniqueness of the doctrine of the Trinity   73
    The Great Benediction and my tepid attention   76
    Chaplain trainees ask questions   77
    Turning to devotional life with the Trinity   78
    Being led into Jesus's great commandment   82
    Transcending words   83
    So what? What difference does it make?   83
    A vast treasure-house   84

Glossary   87

Bibliography   93

Foreword

Dr. Ralph Reeves is perhaps one of the most generative thinkers I know. It has been my privilege to have known Ralph, and have been in "dialogue" with him now for 30 years. Ralph and I first met in the Fall of 1990 when I attended, by invitation of another, a social gathering at Ralph's home. These gathers, known as Luther and Lager or L&L , became something of a home for me during my first year of life and practice in Reading, helping to cut the loneliness of spending that first year away from my wife, two sons and new born daughter. It was in this setting that Ralph invited me to take a Saturday walk with him up on the Hawk Mountain Sanctuary. Hawk Mountain is right on the Eastern Flyway for migrating birds of prey, and a spectacular, if physically demanding hike, especially for me who, at the time, was in great need of a total hip replacement. The conversation that day ranged over many themes and topics central of which were Carlos Castaneda's *The Teachings of Don Juan*, and Paulo Friere's *Pedagogy of the Oppressed*. The conversation and the hike had the quality for me of having grabbed hold of a force that both pulled me along and bid me keep up. So began a friendship that is both intellectually stimulating and relationally invigorating.

At the time of Ralph's retirement from hospital in-patient practice in 2005, then Chief of Psychiatry, Dr. Larry Rotenberg, called me to ask if I might be willing to have Ralph as a paid consultant to the Clinical Pastoral Education Program. I was delighted by the offer and gladly accepted. Ralph began attending a weekly seminar (in that CPE program) called a Verbatim Seminar. During this seminar chaplains in training present conversations they have had with hospital patients. These cases, usually difficult, involve word for word accounts of the chaplain/patient dialogue. This allows the seminar participants to engage the presenter regarding their working assumptions, experience and emotions and their reflections on the deeper content and meaning of the encounter. This often leads to theological reflection by all. Ralph found these seminars deeply enjoyable and stimulating. Ralph and I had already established a weekly lunch meeting, but the verbatim seminars opened up a new line conversation, Ralph's effort to describe the results of effective dialogue. I think it was here that the "Dialogue Project" which became this book gained focus and began in earnest.

This book is the product of a concerted effort on Ralph's part to engage a goal that he initially described as inducing people to love one another better. Ralph Reeves is not your typical American School Psychiatrist. He was first trained in psycho-dynamically oriented therapy, but later he came to more deeply value the mutuality of interaction with his patients. Consequently, while he knows the medicine of psychiatry, he is most interested in the effects conversation has with his patients, the meanings formed between him and them—co-created between him and them—and the resultant growth and recovery. This paying attention to how his interaction affects a patient led Ralph to the conclusion that effective dialogue can be gauged by the occurrence of new meanings as they arise from the co-operation of the two partners in dialogue.

These meanings have a persisting quality that give them a potency beyond the immediate effect on the two in dialogue. Ralph came to give a name to this co-created dialogue, calling it "co-dialogue," and to the peaks of these co-created meanings, calling them "co-statements." He concluded that the occurrence of a co-statement was an observable sign of effective dialogue.

If you know Ralph Reeves, you also know he is not inclined to limit his reflection to the clinical interaction. Ralph also noticed that co-dialogue seemed a reflection of another deeper reality, that of Trinity. Here is where Ralph has really challenged my thinking as a theologically trained professional. Ralph sees good dialogue as a reflection of the interaction of the Godhead as expressed in the Christian symbol for Trinity. His willingness to think theologically is consistent with his own spirituality, and is not intended to exclude those of a different view, but rather to grasp something of the eternal dynamism of Holy interaction, both immanent and transcendent, in a way that will advance healthy loving relationships in general.

I hope you will be as challenged and edified by this brief monograph as I have been, as I have been one of several sounding boards for Ralph through many years of lively dialogue with him as my good friend and consultant.

GREGORY ALAN STODDARD, MDIV, DMIN, CE
Greg Stoddard is an Ordained Lutheran Pastor and Certified Educator with the Association for Clinical Pastoral Education. He served as Department and Program Director for Chaplaincy and Clinical Pastoral Education at The Reading Hospital—Tower Health where he was the CPE program founder. He currently serves as Interim Doctor of Ministry Program Director at Union Theological Seminary in New York City.

When you and I talk, surprising wonderful things can happen for both of us. And WE-hood can occur.

When you and anybody talk, surprising wonderful things can happen for both for you. And WE-hood can occur.

Chapter 1

Celebrating Relationships

THIS IS A BOOK about relationships. I believe that we all, especially me, are in need of good relationships, and a great many of us don't have them. Here we start by celebrating seven moments of psychotherapy dialogue in which relationship was so good that it left a "footprint in time" in the form of a unique statement. The occurrence of such a statement carried great meaning, and was an indicator of new hope and also of a particular verbal kind of love between the partners in the dialogue. It brought benefits to both partners. Such statements can bring benefits to you, too, as you read of them.

We can characterize relationship in the phrase "You-I-You-I-OH!," as each partner discovers the other partner, step by step, and experiences wonderful surprises: "OH!" As they discover each other more and more deeply, they can enjoy their developing "WE-hood." They come to recognize that the effects of their dialogue are desirable for both of them. These desirable results occur not so much because they are desired or striven for. They are not caused by an attempt to answer questions. Rather, they occur because of the freedom of spontaneous expression in grace. In the field of grace, cause-and-effect are transcended; striving also is transcended. Grace is a free gift. This is true for human grace and graciousness, as well as divine grace and graciousness. Thus, unexpected but desirable new meanings can emerge: unearned, surprising, refreshing, gratifying.

As a psychiatrist and psychotherapist, I have been very fortunate to be a part of some of this WE-hood, and the surprising wonderful statements that happen in it, and the sense of grace that accompanies it. In a sense, this whole book is written to honor my patients, especially those who have spoken such statements. In a therapy session, one of us (usually the patient) makes an unusual kind of statement that arises not from either partner individually, but from the relationship itself. It is not merely an "I" statement, or a "you" statement; it is a "WE"-statement. That is, it contains references to meanings that have been contributed by both partners. So I say that it is co-created, and I call it a co-statement.

My earlier publication described these "co-statements" in a briefer, more academic way.[1]

USING ACTUAL QUOTES

Most writing on relationship offers generalizations about it. But here, we will use actual quotes of wonderful things that actually were spoken in psychotherapy sessions. Here is one of them. A patient whom I shall call Diane (not her real name) said: "You made me feel important yesterday, even when you were mad with me."

On first glance, this may not appear to be a profoundly important statement, especially if you are not a psychotherapist. But we will delve rather deeply into it and show its importance. Just the mention of importance and anger in the same statement is quite unusual and powerful for psychotherapy.

I will present seven such statements and discuss each one and the qualities that make it profoundly full of meaning, especially meaning about the relationship from which it emerged. Each of these statements is unique to its particular psychotherapy session. But each one also expresses a much broader quality of humanness. We could even call it wisdom. Indeed, the human wisdom of each

---

1. Reeves, "The Co-Statement."

statement is such that it could have been spoken by many other persons who have no contact with the statement's origin, but who may have had an experience of a similar configuration of meanings. (A side benefit of this broad general humanness is that none of these statements could ever be used to discern the identity of any particular speaker.)

In each co-statement, both my patient and I were enriched with deepened meanings and mutuality, producing this specifically verbal form of love. I hope that you too will find that these considerations enrich your relationships, and your humanity and your love. Indeed, you may even be brought to recall some parallel issue in your own life that you wish you could speak of to someone in heartful relationship.

These surprising statements are quite rare in my experience. We will explore their occurrence and their nature and their complex meanings. And we will ask what it is about the field of dialogue that makes it even possible for them to occur. Their very occurrence enriches our understanding of relationship, communication, language, even love and fruitfulness and relational wisdom.[2]

---

2. Far back in 1979, I had the privilege of reading Teilhard de Chardin's great book, *The Phenomenon of Man*. Recently, I picked up that book again, and I was astounded to see that very much of my present approach to dialogue has a structure of meaning with strong echoes of Teilhard. That is to say that Teilhard's book produced a radical change in my entire meaning system, even though I did not realize it at the time. The following quote from him seems to me to give clear evidence of such echoes in regard to my study of the field of co-dialogue and the co-statement. That is, in this quote, Teilhard's words are directly applicable to the question of what makes it possible for the field of dialogue to occur. "[In the occurrence of the co-statement, we are given] to discover the universal hidden beneath the exceptional. . . . [Such an] irregularity in nature is only the sharp exacerbation, to the point of perceptible disclosure, of a property of things diffused throughout the universe, in a state which eludes our recognition of its presence. Properly observed, even if only in one spot, a phenonmenon [such as a co-statement] necessarily has an omnipresent value and roots by reason of the fundamental unity of the world" (*Phenomenon*, 55–56).

The Specific Relationship-Statements:

Each statement is from a different patient. It emerged during one of my therapy sessions with that patient. Each statement has been *recognized* as important and lifted out of its original context. I emphasize the act of recognizing, because I am convinced that such statements occur much more often than they are recognized.

1. Carol: "My pastor never talked to me like that (*viz.*, like you just did), but I always thought he ought to give up pastoring and become a sportscaster."
2. Diane: "You made me feel important yesterday, even when you were mad with me."
3. Emily: If you don't trust me, doesn't that mean that you want to get rid of me?
4. Frances: It would be easier to give you my body than my mind.
5. Therapist to Johnny: "What are we going to work on today?"
   Johnny: "It's not what are *we* going to work on; it's what am *I* going to work on."
6. Therapist to Roland: "It's time to think about how you are going to use me today."
   Roland immediately said: "That sounds like prostitution!"
   Soon after, without any therapist intervention, Roland said: "Aha! Prostitution is sex without commitment; therapy is commitment without sex!"
7. Thomas: "Last week, you answered my questions in a way that did not make me feel stupid, but made me feel smart. So I figured I could tell you these things (his history of terrible life experiences)."

Each of these co-statements has significant powers:

1. Each one has power to affect you personally, as you ponder it. Each one also still affects me personally, as I ponder it.
2. Each one has the power, in itself, to lead you into imagining some aspects of its origin in the original relationship, without your knowing its actual history.

3. Each one has certain meanings about relationship, love, and hope, that can be inferred from the free-standing statement itself, even when it is taken out of its context of origin.
4. Each one has power to connect with broader realms of human studies and experience.

THE FIELD: MYSTERY, PRESENCE, AND OPENNESS

Let us consider some qualities of the field in which these statements occur. The first quality is mystery. All relationship takes place as mystery. One person, who is already a complex mystery in him/her self, encounters another person, who is also a complex mystery, and they may become unified into a unique relationship of two, which is a far more complex mystery. In addition, there is mystery in the fact that some of that uniqueness is also consummate humanness, and can carry over to have broad significance for others in their own relationships. All of this takes place in a "field" of dialogue.

The second quality is presence. In psychotherapy, there is interaction using words, with a lot of listening to each other. This listening may consist of deep emptying by the listener. That emptying of one's self somehow makes one's presence more powerful, so that it evokes openness in the partner. As one gives emptiness, one then becomes able to receive fully. So we say that there is a lot of giving and receiving of deep meanings with each other. In my experience, such giving and receiving is essentially effortless, and occurs as grace in the field of dialogue. Much more about that later. The mode of the process is that each partner will be fully present to the other as much as possible. In that full presence, they are much more likely to transcend "small talk" and speak from their souls. They will enjoy sharing the mysteries of their relationship, and thus undergo "healing through meeting." Their dialogue will bear fruit, which can contribute to the healing of others who had no connection with its origins!

A third quality is radical openness to speaking one's own soul, and to being empty enough to receive the soul-speak of the partner—thus to be genuinely affected by the partner's speaking his/her soul. We will see more about this as we go along. (I may say that I have never urged anyone to be open, or to trust me. In my view, openness and trust arise from good listening and good presence, not from persuasion or urging.)

YOUR CHOICES

Let's take a moment to distinguish between two major styles of approaching this material. You may find yourself either more devotional-oriented, or more event-and-science oriented. If you are more devotional-oriented, then you may notice that a dialogue process like this has much to suggest "spirit," an indwelling spirit of interaction. You might want to begin with chapter 6, which I call "a pointer to the Trinity," and chapter 7, where we take for granted the spiritual significance of these co-statements, and consider calling in a spiritual ideal. We will use Christian images because I am much more familiar with those. Thus, we will "call in the Holy Trinity" into our dialogue relationship. You can later take up the basic events between humans that are discussed in chapters 2–6. You will see that a fuller understanding of these verbal events between humans does point to spirit. Such an understanding points from psychotherapy relationships toward divine relationships, such as those imputed to the Trinity, and toward inviting the Trinity to join our relationships.

If you are event-and-science oriented, you should go to chapter 2, which describes the several unique statement-events that I have selected for this study. I have given each of the patients fictitious names: Diane, Carol, Emily, Frances, Johnny, Roland, and Thomas. There is one statement for each of the seven different patients. Each event occurred as a fruit of our relationship, manifested in a particular statement that has very unusual and powerful meaning-properties. These chapters are designed to lead to chapter 7, where we will see what it might mean to "call in the Trinity" into those relationships.

Chapter 6 presents a personal moment that I call "Tum Tose." That is baby-talk for "come close." It occurred when I was a toddler.

The structure of this incident has three persons: my mother and my father and me. The obvious loving that is going on in that event is so powerful that it points to the operation of the Christian Trinity, and lays a groundwork for chapter 7.

Chapter 7 has the form of a guided meditation on divine human relationships. It suggests that in our human dialogues we can become joined to a divine being-structure and gain deepening of our dialogues. Thus, we may come to a relationship that is simultaneously divine and human.

We will do this through joining the Holy Trinity of Christianity. This combination of human and divine dimensions presents mystery on several levels. You may benefit from this guided meditation as a dream of an ideal, even if you don't believe in the Trinity.

According to some versions of Christian theology, the Trinity is explicitly eager to join us, to indwell us, while also we are willing to call in and receive It/Them. (This awkward expression is meant to preserve our awareness that the Trinity is/are simultaneously One and Three. From now on, I will use the plural form, for simplicity of expression.) While many ideals may benefit the dialogical relationship, I find the Trinity to be the most helpful and powerful, as a kind of template for loving interaction. If you know of other divine structures that can be used for this purpose, I am eager to know about them.

You may also benefit if you become joined to other ideals, such as those of humanism. Those ideals, too, can be "called in" to augment and deepen our relationships. For instance, one or both partners may call in Buber's "I-thou"[3] relationship as an ideal. But I am not familiar with any humanistic ideal that actively offers itself to us as the Trinity are said to do.

May all your relationships be filled with love: effortless, grace-filled giving and receiving of meaning and love between you and your dialogue partners, plus the love that overflows so liberally from the relationships among the persons of the Holy Trinity, and flows into our human-human loving to make it divine.

3. Buber, *I and Thou*, 39.

Chapter 2

Meeting the Co-creators

THIS CHAPTER CONTAINS DESCRIPTIONS of the seven different co-statements and how each of them came to be. The first and second ones, Diane's and Carol's, are described rather extensively. The others are described more briefly. All of them share certain properties, which I will detail.

DIANE

We have already met Diane in the first chapter. As you will recall, she said: "Doctor, you made me feel important yesterday, even when you were mad at me." You can already see that Diane had some severe problems with anger—mainly at being the recipient of it. She seems surprised to recognize that she had never before felt important during an angry encounter. So you can see that this one statement alone carries profound meanings about our relationship, and about other contrasting relationships in her life. It prescribes a large part of her future treatment. She seems ready to expand her learning about feeling important even in other situations where there is anger. We can already see that this combination of anger and importance is hugely human, and could be claimed by many other people.

Meeting the Co-creators

This was *her* interpretation, not mine. My memory of that meeting on the previous day included no awareness of being angry with her, or of trying to make her feel important. All this happened during a hospital admission for depression. On the third day, I had had to address her failure to attend the several group therapies. So I gave her my usual lecture on the importance of those therapies. She took our interaction and processed it in herself and came up with her own new interpretation of it, derived from her own life experiences. And she had the courage and gumption to bring her interpretation back and present it to me. (She might not have been so open. She might have kept it secret.)

In her statement, she referred to things that I had said and done. Referring implicitly to my lecture to her about attending groups, she asserted that I was angry with her. In doing so, she included not only meanings from me, but also some that had come to her about herself: the joining of anger and importance. Since meanings from both of us were included, I say that the statement was created by both of us. It was "co-created."

She made that statement more than twenty years ago. While other nuances of the session have faded over time, the power and import of her statement for me have not diminished. It is still imprinted on my memory as clearly as the day she said it. And I still honor her for speaking it.

I might have been so deep in my pompous hospital psychiatrist mode that I would have failed to notice her statement's power. I might have said: "Don't tell me about that. Just go to the groups." But I have always been very grateful that I did notice it and use it in the dialogues with her; and I also saved it for study later, even now. It impelled me to look for such statements of power in other relationships. And that has led to this project which I am sharing now with you.

As we study it now, we find several dimensions that are worth noting.

1. Her statement clearly had interpersonal properties. It connected us. It arose from our relationship, and it is a kind of fruit of our interaction. Often in a dialogue, someone deliberately

attempts to summarize the dialogue through some conscious sharing or agreement between the partners. That may lead to a statement of the form: "This is what I hear you saying . . ." But that was not at all the intention of Diane's statement. Rather, it arises from some much more surprising depth of mental processing. It points to a perceived difference between us (e.g., that I was mad with her). And it begins to heal that difference, by announcing that she feels important anyway. It gives the feel of newness, like an "Aha!"

2. Her statement indicates things not only about her, and not only about me, but also about the state of our connection, our "therapeutic relationship." It was one in which both of us were listening and responding, and allowing our selves to be affected by each other. I was affected with a certain excitement, as I scrambled to grasp the full import of her bringing that statement. She was affected by feeling important in spite of her sense that I was angry. Given the fact that we were both affected simultaneously and beneficially, we can say that there was mutuality between us.

3. Her statement opened very important issues of her treatment, issues that we had not yet discussed. How was she to handle her fears that I might get angry with her? How could we work together?

4. Her statement offered a solution to those questions. That is, she engaged with me in such a way that she felt important anyway.

5. Her statement unified anger and importance in a way that was new and very useful. That combination was new to my understanding, as well as to hers. Maybe it is new to you too.

6. She had the courage to present her formulation, which was a very unconventional way of relating to me.

7. She gave her statement freely, as a revelation of herself, given with "no strings attached." That is, she exhibited no defensiveness; instead, she opened herself to whatever response I would make.

8. Her statement had so much meaning, so much power in meaning, even so much *being*, that it can be extracted from

that dialogue and studied on its own, abstractly, as we are doing now. Having such being, it can go out into the world on its own, and have beneficial effects upon many people.
9. With this amount of meaning-power *in mutuality*, we can say that a verbal interaction like this is one form of love.
10. We can now speak of one of the sparkling facets of her co-statement. She speaks the soul of the relationship at that moment. When such a statement of self-revealing occurs, I call it "soul-speak." Unfortunately, we may sometimes implicitly assume that soul-speak is not a relational thing, but rather that it has to do with one person who is speaking his/her soul. That is, we might assume that it is monadic, like a soliloquy. However, for us here, soul-speak is not merely coming from one soul. Rather, it occurs in a field of co-dialogue, and its nature is that it also is simultaneously aimed toward another soul. It is one consummation of the relationship. Both partners engage each other from their deepest values, their "souls," in fitting ways, and respond to each other's soul-speak in kind. This is a very special field of relationship.

BROADER REALMS FOR DIANE'S CO-STATEMENT

Surprisingly, Diane's co-statement describes not only her and me; it also describes the Jews, in their biblical history. Although she showed no indication of intending to broaden the meaning, her co-statement in the abstract turns out to be a great description of the Jews' experience of their God, as described in the Hebrew Scriptures. God was often very angry with them—but in being so, he also made them feel important—even chosen.

My personal life also echoes Diane's co-statement. Many years after she made her co-statement, I came to realize that her statement described my relationship with my own father. In my psychoanalysis, I came to realize that the times when I felt closest to him—most important to him—were the times when he was angry and was spanking me (while simultaneously apologizing to me: "Son, this hurts me a lot more than it hurts you!").

Even now, her co-statement may be "contagious," like a "meaning-virus." You may "catch" the meaning, and thus be connected with both Diane and me. Thus, her statement is, for us now, an invitation to use our imaginations and memories to re-produce a quality of relationship like that between her and me, uniting anger and importance. That may lead to feelings in you about situations in your own life that join anger and importance, and to some healing of the conflict. It may also lead to your memories of patients who have been in such a situation. Or you may recall situations in literature or theater in which anger and importance are joined.

In contrast to Diane, another patient, "Barbara," made a statement that explicitly separates anger from importance. Speaking of anger at her boy-friend, she said: "Hmph! I just want to get it off my chest. I don't want to have to worry about whether he is listening." It is as if she said, "When I am angry at him, I can't at the same time treat him as important."

Occasionally, I find someone who feels very angry with God but is afraid to say so. Recently I realized that Diane's co-statement sheds some light on the question of what it might mean to be angry with God. This would seem to be closely related to the question of how important one believes that God is—or how important he would be after one expresses anger at him. If anger at someone seems to be equivalent to *obliterating* their importance, as with the example of Diane's co-statement, then this process would feel very different from the opposite condition: if anger at someone is part of *connecting* and *affirming* their importance.

FAILURES AT CO-CREATION

Let us compare a hypothetical "ordinary" dialogue:

1. Patient: "Well, I stopped my medication."
2. Therapist: "Oh. How did you decide to do that?"
3. Patient: "I went to a conference on natural healing."
4. Therapist: "Did you tell your wife about it?"
5. Patient: "Oh, no. I just wanted to try something different on my own."

6. Therapist: "A sense of needing more independence? . . ."
7. Patient: "I was afraid you would be upset with me."
8. Therapist: "Oh. You shouldn't worry about that."

The flow of meanings here is typical of many of the interchanges in would-be psychotherapy sessions. Each statement conveys a simple meaning, and a certain meaning-load. But none of these statements or responses have much effect on the relationship, or on the meaning-flow of the ongoing dialogue. "Healing through meeting" requires a convergence of meanings in the ongoing dialogue. But here, this little dialogue does not offer that kind of convergence. Indeed, the therapist's last comment really does nothing to deepen the relationship, and actually destroys meaning and convergence.

Also, as you can see, none of these ordinary statements even approach the relational power that Diane's co-statement has. After her co-statement, the flow of meanings and the convergence between her and me will develop dramatically, and with little effort.

This hypothetical dialogue contains certain words that could have been occasions for expanding the flow of meaning. The word "medication" could invite discussion of effectiveness of treatment, or side effects or cost. The word "independence" could resonate with past discussions of him and his wife and issues of dependency or co-dependency. The words "afraid" and "upset" offer a large variety of possibilities for exploring broader issues. The therapist's rather vapid reassurance is a real conversation-stopper. It may indicate that therapist had some "counter-transference" to the patient's stopping the medication.

Unsatisfying Conversations:

There are of course many other conversational relationships which are not satisfying. In many conversations, the pattern is one of competition. One person expresses his/her point of view, then the partner expresses a contrasting point of view. The first person argues with the partner, and they engage in disagreements until there is anger, or change of subject. Maybe they "agree to disagree." Or one partner may give up and say, in defeat, "OK, I see that you are right."

In these cases, real "listening" with mutual openness is nearly absent, and trivialities and ignorings and arguments occur. In these, each partner fails to manifest vulnerability to being affected constructively by the other partner. And they do not produce fruitful statements of high degrees of meaning and being.

DIANE'S LIFE FUNCTIONS: FRUIT AND SEED

In contrast to those unsatisfying conversations, we now consider the satisfactions of noticing fruit and seed, the "life functions" that manifest in Diane's co-statement and the other ones. I have claimed that a co-statement is both a fruit of the partners' deep meaning and mutuality, and a seed for the occurrence of further meaning and mutuality. We know, of course, that fruit and seed are functions of living beings. How can two such life functions exist in a mere statement, no matter how special?

1. We see that two living beings are involved in its co-creation; so it should not be too surprising that it has some functions like those of living beings.
2. After the statement has come into being, it is free-standing, like a fruit. It can exist like an apple, independently of its origin. And it beckons to be tasted.
3. Beyond that, it also feeds back to comment upon the relationship from which it arose, and also to modulate that relationship as it continues. That is, it seeds the subsequent relationship. That produces new insight, not only in the partners, but also in observers like you who are witnessing it.

Fruit of Relationship Heals:

This fruit of the relationship with Diane is a piece of wisdom which embodies and remembers a healing moment, a peak moment, in our relationship. It had to do with realizing the possibility of experiencing anger and importance together, and the healing that accompanied that. For Carol, it was her acknowledging that she really could be affected in a positive way. For Emily, the healing occurred in her challenging me about her fear that I would reject her—kick her out of treatment. You can see that the other co-statements also heal a distance between us. They heal a conflict which previously had gone unrecognized. Clearly each co-statement (except Johnny's) arises from a process of interaction which fosters closeness and understanding and positive feelings. We can recognize this process as one way of loving one another.

A Seed for Wisdom Literature:

Let me propose a thought experiment. Imagine your favorite bulletin board where wisdom quotes are set out. I dare say that all the wisdom that you have ever seen on wisdom boards has been monadic wisdom: the self-contained sage makes a pronouncement, an injunction, an "ought to love . . ." But it is not thereby an inducement for a loving relationship, because it is a kind of command, and it may produce resistance. With Diane, we have a set of powerful meaning-full statements which, if posted on a wisdom board, could instead give the reader not a command to obey, but a seed, an invitation to enter into a similar kind of mutuality—a similar kind of love!

Talk About Dialogue vs. Talk in Dialogue:

There is much good literature that tells quite well *about* dialogue, but does not give examples of actual words that were uttered *in* the dialogue. Anderson[1] offers one such excellent description.

In contrast, I have been emphasizing the importance of the actual statements of patients. Diane's co-statement, as we see, does have a great deal of meaning and power of relationship, and it produced fruit that we are enjoying at this moment. As we also saw, it has a great deal of meaning in realms beyond interpersonal relationships. Now, I present six more co-statements, considered more briefly than Diane's.

1. Anderson, "Listening, Hearing and Speaking."

Celebrating This Power of Word:

As I share with you, I want to celebrate this power of Word, and to celebrate these pieces of good news with Diane and Carol and Emily and the others. What a surprise it has been to me, as they have unfolded in my life over the last few decades! They represent a whole realm of very positive experiences that I had not known how to notice or attend to. But now I do know (at least sometimes).

FOCUSING ON CAROL AND HER HISTORY

In one sense, you don't need any help in enjoying a jewel, especially a living jewel like that co-statement of Diane's. But let me give you some other examples, starting with Carol (not her real name). After all of the examples, I will point out important similarities among them (in chapter 3).

Carol was a middle-aged woman who came into the hospital for depression. Her husband had died many years earlier, and she felt very unloved. She presented many of the typical symptoms of depression. But one unusual symptom was that she felt "dried up and cut off." She told me that she was a Christian, and she had been praying for improvement, but had gotten none. After several days in hospital, we discharged her to office appointments. She came to the first one and said: "I don't know what I am doing here. You can't help me. I am just all dried up and cut off."

I had heard her use that phrase several times, as she catalogued her symptoms of depression. I had had a subtle sense of connection with that particular phrase. But this time, I got fully connected with it. I remembered that it came from the biblical book of Ezekiel, chapter 37, the famous vision of the dry bones. Ezekiel hears God say: "Son of man, can these bones live" (Ezek 37:3 KJV)? ". . . the whole house of Israel . . . say, Our bones are dried, and our hope is lost; we are clean cut off" (Ezek 37:11 RSV). In the vision, God goes on to restore the dry bones to life. After some reflection, and because she was a Christian, I decided to read the vision to her. After I read it, I said: "You are not acting like you believe in that story."

Immediately, she said: "My pastor never talked to me like that (i.e., like you just did). But I always thought he ought to give up pastoring and be a sportscaster!" Just as Diane did, we see that Carol constructed a single statement that referred to meanings that had come from me (i.e., how I talked with her), and also meanings that had come from her, such as her surprise and consternation, and her disappointment in her pastor. And Carol spoke immediately, spontaneously. More importantly for her treatment, she strongly implied in this statement that she had been affected positively by my challenge to receive hope from this vision of Ezekiel.

As with Diane, Carol's co-statement literally produced a new quality of connection and grace and mutuality between her and me. It not only occurred as a momentary event in our field of interaction, but it also continued to affect that field. It was like the proverbial almond tree: it shed its fragrance upon all subsequent statements by either her or me.

As if to say "I can be affected":

We can integrate and paraphrase what happened in the field of that relationship. It is as if she were to respond: "Now I can see that I am not, after all, a person who cannot be affected by some positive message. And I see that you can see that too." Interestingly, this could be a definition of a peak of mutuality: the gracious convergence of differences in perspective. This verbal interaction could, like Diane's, be one form of verbal love.

Her co-statement will feed back to affect her and me and the field of our relationship and the field of you readers plus me. Her statement is so strong with both meaning and power, that it can take on a being of its own, an independence of its own, just as Diane's. And both statements can go out into the world to affect others, including you at this very moment.

Let us look at it now in its context for you. As with Diane's, it carries its own evidence that it arose out of a relationship, and it offers evidence of mutuality, and of its being co-created. That co-createdness equipped it with the power to convey itself to others.

You can "catch" some mutuality from hearing it. It created a new field that included me and her, but now includes you too.

Thus, it functions like a seed. It suggests consolations to many who have been disappointed by a therapist or pastor or other leader—to any who may not have realized that anything better was available. And it emboldens those who have silently tolerated pastors who do not fully profess their calling. Perhaps there were times when you yourself were pleasantly surprised by a helpful message from an unexpected source, which created new hope in you; or the opposite: when someone failed to offer needed, expectable inspiration, and instead offered you the "wisdom" of the sportscaster.

The co-statement has *being*. It was co-created in the field of interaction, and it has being enough that we can extract it from that field for our purposes here, and study it as a free-standing entity. It reveals that she and I, as partners, are unified into a single complex system of interaction. In that system, we have ongoing effects upon each other, and these effects are mutually beneficial.

UNIFICATION AND SPIRIT: HOW MIGHT SCIENCE SIMULATE THIS?

This is, then, another instance of the unification of parts into a single grander system. It occurs so often that we can give it a name. We can call it "spirit." How can we understand this? Perhaps only by participating in it, as we are doing now. It is a mystery that will someday be addressed by the budding science of complex systems, mentioned above. So we can wonder how that science will simulate this episode of spirit and unification and mutually agreeable affecting of each other. See chapter 4: "How does it work?"

THE POWER OF WORDS

Surely, science will posit the immense power of words to produce the mutual effects in such a system. Carol's co-statement is very powerful, as it expresses her ability to let herself be affected in a positive way, in mutuality by another person and also by words from Scripture—and by the conjunction of a person (me) and a Scripture. In addition to her co-statement, her story also gives us another example of the power of words. The scriptural words "dried up and cut off" have great power for those who have been exposed to Ezekiel's vision. In Carol, their meaning had shrunk to fit the symptoms of depression. She had apparently forgotten their connection with the hope-filled vision of Ezekiel. But those words, when said to me yet again, obviously had the power to trigger my own memory of that vision, and in turn, to restore her own connection with that story of hope.

EMILY: "SO I WON'T HAVE TO LIE"

Emily was a young woman who had rather severe issues of trust and belonging and compliance, especially with medications. Once in a meeting with several staff, she commented: "I always try to take my medications on the day I am coming to see the doctor, so I won't have to lie about it." (How many other patients have said something very similar!)

When I heard that statement, I realized that it was actually a piece of self-revelation. It was something of a dare, and possibly an indication that she was accessible to talk about issues of trust. I said: "If you're going to treat me like that, I don't know how I can trust you." The conversation went on to other issues. A few days later, she came in for her regular individual session. She started with her co-statement: "If you don't trust me, doesn't that mean that you want to get rid of me?" In that one statement, she packed meanings about her three core issues: trust, belonging, and compliance.

I assured her that I did not want to get rid of her. If I had been at my best, I would have summarized my feelings and response to her by saying: "No, I don't want to get rid of you. I want to hold on to you until you become trustworthy—not only to me but to your own self." I was not so eloquent at the time. Nevertheless, her statement carried many new meanings for us, and opened the field for many subsequent new meanings, especially about trust and attachment and their opposites.

Exploring Emily's Co-statement:

Let us explore Emily's co-statement in terms of the criteria that we have used above with Diane.

1. It is clearly co-created, as it expresses material from both of us: my comment about trusting her, and her fears of being rejected.
2. It is clearly free-standing, as we are now studying it in a place far from its origin.
3. It points to a difference between us, and it lays out that difference so clearly that it suggests a solution. Her implied solution is that I would decline to reject her.
4. We can see that her urgent question served to modulate our relationship of trust *vs.* mistrust.
5. Regarding newness, both of her statements seem to offer a new dare, a testing of our relationship (which had been well-tested on several occasions before).

Other Similar Patients:

Many persons have been in similar dilemmas. Indeed, many of those who are abused as children have reported the abuse and because of that very reporting they have been treated as untrustworthy and rejectable. This statement resonates with many dimensions of the so-called "borderline personality." A very famous book about that condition is called, "*I hate you. Don't leave me.*" That title suggests dynamics that we see in force in Emily's co-statement. We could paraphrase that title to fit with her: "I lied to you; don't reject me."

The Christian Bible:

Her co-statement also resonates with a part of the Christian Bible, which offers an opposite response to un-trust-worthiness. Paul says this: "While we were yet sinners Christ died for us" (Rom 5:8 KJV). That is, while we were yet untrustworthy, Christ did not want to reject us, but rather he wanted to draw us in and give himself for us. (If any of you know of similar messages in other religions, please enjoy them, and let me know about them.) Emily's co-statement can be seen as an urgent request for that very assurance. Her co-statement-as-question resonates with many who are caught between trust and distrust or between acceptance and rejection.

FRANCES ON GIVING HERSELF

Frances' co-statement says: "It would be easier to give you my body than my mind." I have chosen to present this one late in this series, because many hearers who have not been introduced to intimate issues in psychotherapy think immediately of a bar scene, and consider her statement to be a proposition for unethical behavior. As such, it would not be worthy of our attention in this context. But its powers are very much like those of the other co-statements. We can observe that it offers new framings of our relationship, and it also takes the form of a by-word for many who have been abused, and who have thus been led to separate their body from their mind. It is well-known that persons being abused often "go somewhere else in their mind" at those times. Those are unfortunate people, engaged in a terrible struggle. They find it easier to give their body—to submit to an event of the violation of their body—rather than to allow themselves to commit what feels like a violation of the sovereignty of their mind and their personhood. Incidentally, this suggests one pathway for the development of a dissociative process, which could develop from such abuse.

Frances was a woman who suffered from depression, which she herself connected to sexual abuse of her by her father many years earlier. In its origin, this co-statement was a meta-communication which bespoke the soul of our relationship. She was depressed, but she was by this time living a rather healthy life, with a good relationship with her husband and children, and was active in her church. Her statement occurred after about two years of therapy, during which she had come to know clearly that I was not about to engage in any unethical behaviors with her. Her co-statement was a brilliant summary of many months of therapeutic relationship, and some transference issues. It was a major focusing of conflicting issues from the past, leading up to that moment. And it pointed to what needed to be worked on in subsequent months of therapy; namely, her intense fear of giving too much of her mind, revealing too much too fast in the therapeutic efforts.

Connecting with Other Realms:

We have already described the connection of this statement with many persons who have been sexually abused, and with their treatment. This statement also resonates curiously with one version of Christian theology. Christ found it too difficult to give his disciples his mind; that is, to get them to cognitively understand him and his teaching and preaching and counseling. So he taught them by giving them his body and blood, his actions in the world, first in bread and wine, in his Last Supper; and then in flesh in great suffering and dying through crucifixion! What better way for us to learn something new about dying?

TALKING ABOUT OUR RELATIONSHIP ITSELF: JOHNNY, ROLAND, AND THOMAS

Below we will consider three more statements of high relational power. Each one actually comes as a pair of statements. Each of them was an important turning point in the therapy. And you can feel that the patient and I were unified in the process of interaction, which also included some conflict. Each one constitutes an important step in the treatment, but the "flavor" of the mutuality between us is of a different quality from that of the earlier four co-statements.

Johnny: The Question of Who is Doing the Work Here:

Some time ago, I made a statement early in a therapy session with Johnny. I said, "What are we going to work on today?"

The patient, about forty years old, in his second year of treatment in a partial hospital program for severely persistently mentally ill persons, responded: "It's not what are *we* going to work on; it's what am *I* going to work on."

He thereby reveals an important meaning-awareness: his isolation, and his "model" of me as an obstruction to his treatment. And he gives me confirmation of my model of him as someone with profound conflicts about receiving help and treatment. Thus, his statement is a very useful model of our relationship, and indeed grows out of our relationship. In other words, he spontaneously set us in a "ball park" that gave us a major "permission" to work on one of his core issues: his ambivalence about receiving any effects from me or from the treatment team.

Roland and the Therapist's Error:

Roland was about twenty-four years old. At the beginning of our session, he engaged in distractions as he often did, using materials that are kept on my desk for that purpose. After several minutes of that, I was feeling impatient, and I said: "It's time to think about how you are going to use me today."

He immediately said: "That sounds like prostitution!"

What an expressive way to comment on his conflicts about our relationship! And on my having missed the appropriate "ball park" for our work on that day. After his uncomplimentary assertion, I analyzed my own statement and I realized that I had forgotten reports that he was struggling with some issues about his wishing for—and dreading—emotional closeness with me, along with some possible doubts about his sexual orientation. How could I forget such a thing? In my statement, I had unintentionally and indirectly alluded to those very subjects! However, I fortunately followed good technique and made no attempt to defend myself or to repair the field. A few minutes later, he spontaneously exclaimed: "Aha! Prostitution is sex without commitment; therapy is commitment without sex!"

In so saying, Roland offered his own repair of the mutuality in the field. That is, he repaired his initial cynical and fearful statement about prostitution, and also created a piece of wisdom, maybe even a bumper sticker!

I believe that these examples of Johnny and Roland illustrate that the patient and I managed to get onto the same "page," the same "ball park." When this happens, then the patient and I are in an important sense unified. Our meanings meet in edifying ways, and we are both changed in edifying ways. Roland's "Aha" statement is a good example of this, and it also echoes, in humanness, many others who have similar conflicts about closeness. His statement has a lot of relevance to other relationships outside ours.

Modulating Conflict With The Partner:

The two examples above, Johnny and Roland, both bespeak conflict. Perhaps it should be called "transference issues," in the field between the patient and me. (Analysis of the transference is not a common focus in patients with severe persistent mental illness.) We see that the field of wholeness contains ways of modulating such conflicts. For Johnny, it was about his disdain of our efforts to "treat" him, and his long-awaited occasion to speak that disdain. His statement was a permission to address it more directly, to now allow it to be a focus of treatment. For Roland, the conflict was about emotional closeness and the vulnerability to sexual feelings. He stated well his resolution of this, in his statement given above. In each of these cases, new meanings emerged, and each relationship deepened in beneficial ways.

Thomas, Revealing Deep Secrets:

Thomas was in his late twenties, and was also in a program for persistently mentally ill persons. We spent many sessions talking about "the system," and a political agenda focusing on his immense anger about many difficulties he had in foster care and in jail. I "played in his ball park," and actually responded to some of his misunderstandings about the nature of democracy, and the functions of lawyers as differentiated from those of judges, and the existence of many people's attempts to create an improved system for society. He eagerly wrote down some of my statements, especially the word "utopia."

In our next session, with no real prompting from me, he made a large departure from his usual angry complaints about "the system" (the legal and political system, not the mental health system). He told me of some very terrible events in his life in foster care. A week after he told these things, we reflected on how it felt to reveal those things for the first time. He said: "Last week, you answered my questions in a way that did not make me feel stupid, but made me feel smart. So I figured I could tell you these things."

Once again, we note that such conflicts and healings could occur in many therapies. But here is one clear example of their occurrence. Thomas was building and engaging his model of me, as well as of himself, and creating new understandings in the field of our interaction. These consisted at that moment in his realizing that, with some psychosocial support, he could find new ways of handling those memories. He not only exhibited a positive response to my answers to his questions; in addition, he was even able to metacommunicate with me about them! In doing so, he proposed a radically different ball park for his subsequent therapy.

Chapter 3

General Properties of Co-created Statements

EACH OF THESE CO-STATEMENTS occurred during one of a series of psychotherapeutic conversations between the patient and me. No two of them are from the same patient. Four of the patients were suffering from severe persistent mental illness and required years of treatment. Each co-statement carries a high intensity of meaning. The most important criterion for selecting each one is that it spontaneously includes references to meanings that have been contributed by both of us. It also represents a spontaneous win-win in our relationship.

The occurrence of a co-statement gives evidence of several properties as a part of the therapeutic relationship. The patient is:

1. highly involved in the process of therapy.
2. positively affected by the therapy—*and also by the therapist*!
3. clear in acknowledging some previous effects of the therapy—*and the therapist*—upon him/her.
4. highly attentive to significant aspects of our relationship in the present and over time.
5. confident enough to engage in such non-standard kinds of self-report.

6. comfortable enough to bring up potentially painful, conflictual matters about our relationship; and
7. committed to further work in the dialogue in the future.

One might object that not one of these co-statements, taken in itself, indicates that the treatment has already accomplished a high degree of mental healing; not one of them exhibits any effortful deliberate "meeting" nor shared positive regard.

I would argue that these statements are not intended to represent full health, nor the end of treatment; nor even unconditional positive regard between the partners. Rather, each of them represents a solid but thoroughly subjective and relational stepping stone on the pathway to improvement, to "healing through meeting," and an implied reference to deeper more or less unconscious processes and conflicts, *with permission to address them.*

ARTIFICIALLY CONSTRUCTED CO-STATEMENTS

In contrast, Greening[1] has offered examples of statements which were intentionally constructed by him to have properties which might arise from his interpretation of the label "co-statements." These statements may be seen to represent feelings that would be shared, explicitly and deliberately, between two partners—expressing an enviable degree of positive affect, warmth, closeness, affection.

1. "I'm warmed by your caring for me and wishing me a speedy recovery."
2. "I feel close to you when you resonate so closely to my happiness."
3. "Thanks for your sympathy—it helps me feel less alone."
4. "What a relief to learn that you, too, were afraid we were breaking up."

---

1 Greening, personal communication.

THE CO-STATEMENT: BOTH MUTUALITY AND CHALLENGE

While it could be desirable to be in a relationship in which such statements could be made, I would like to reserve the term "co-statement" for statements which include substantial excitement, conflict, "spice," even daring and challenge. They point to not-yet-understood conscious or unconscious feelings and thoughts, simultaneously with the clear implication of being a part of a work in progress, with the qualities described above.

These wonderful moments in dialogue surprise us when we examine their power for meaning and communication and connecting between the dialogue partners, who thus become a WE-hood. The statements address us in a mode that is not one of hierarchy and control. Rather, it is a mode of mutuality, with gracious, freeing interaction and shared meanings. They are unique but also universally human. They are highly relevant to the partners from whom they come, while they also exhibit large amounts of being, and offer connections and messages that can be appreciated and used by many other people, and in several other realms, because they are universally human.

So I claim again that these co-statements offer a clue to the mystery of WE-hood, of mutual, mutually modulated relationship; a clue to the very nature of relationship and word and community and love and spirit. Wisdom is born in such a field of relationship and dialogue.

Chapter 4

Co-dialogue: How Does It Work?

WE ARE CELEBRATING MOMENTS when co-creation is manifested. But also we want to ask what is really going on in the field of interaction that allows such things to happen.

Perhaps my first introduction to such things came from my college English professor, Richard Gunter.

"A GREATER MARVEL"
from *Sentences in Dialogue*, by Richard Gunter

> When speakers make language their sentences come one after another like the links in a chain. A given sentence follows others; it is then itself followed by still others. For some linguists this fact may be simply a bedrock fundamental—something that must be accepted, though it is not itself open to any useful question. But for this writer the chain of sentences has become the most interesting thing about human language. The essays in this little book testify to that interest.
>
> To be more explicit, when people converse they have two roles to play and each role presents two tasks: The roles are PERFORMING and LISTENING; the tasks are MONOLOGUE and DIALOGUE. To perform is to make a sentence, while to listen is simply to entertain

the sentence made by another; monologue is a sequence of sentences, A and B, both made by the same speaker, while dialogue is a sequence in which one speaker makes sentence A and a second makes sentence B. Thus there are four things to do in conversation: One may perform monologue or merely listen to it; and one may perform or listen to dialogue.

These four things may seem very simple, but in fact, though they are not all equally difficult, even the simplest would seem marvelous if it were not so common. It is wonder enough that a speaker can make two sentences and hook them together in monologue so that they seem to him to make sense; it is a greater wonder that he can see coherence in the monologue made by another. But the capacities of the speaker go far beyond the demands of that linguistic task, for he is able to make sentences that respond to sentences made by others. And most wonderful of all, he can even stand passively by as two other minds make sentences back and forth—listen and find sense in their responses to each other. In all the universe that we know, nothing is a greater marvel than that![1]

As we marvel, we will need to make a distinction between my use of the terms interaction vs. relationship. It is a qualitative difference. In the beginning, there may be "resistances" to true relationship. Two people start with an interaction. Either or both of them may feel that he/she is not being affected by the other. And either or both of them may speak without expecting to affect the other or to evoke any soulful response from the other.

But then, the partners get to know each other, perhaps over many sessions. Each one affects the other, and is willing to recognize that he/she is having effects; and each is affected by the other and is willing to recognize his/her being affected. Each one notices the differentnesses of the other, and deepens his/her implicit model of the other. Jane begins to sense some available facets of Bob's self, those aspects that he can give away to her in therapeutic interaction, while still mirroring them in his self. Bob develops the ability to put himself fully into telling his experiences, and thus he is able to give them fully

1. Gunter, *Sentences in Dialogue*, 1–2.

Co-dialogue: How Does It Work?

to Jane. Then we say, as above, that he is speaking both window and mirror. Thus, we are describing an ability *to resonate with one's self while giving to another*. This is one aspect of personhood. Bob similarly senses (probably implicitly) what Jane can give away to him in their interaction—her personhood. And it is not difficult to see how these structures can come together into a co-statement.

Thus, the formation of a co-statement has a dual relationship with time. It arises out of relationship, and also deepens that relationship. As we have seen above, every co-statement includes references to past time, relevance to present time, and pointers to the future. In this sense, we can say that the power of the co-statement both precedes and follows the joining that it produces.

We begin to comprehend the phenomenon of the co-statement as a "nugget" of humanity-in-relationship, actually embodying our success in beneficial interacting. It is a nugget of universal humanity. That is, the "humanity" within which it occurs is precisely the humanity that is not mere individuality but IS relationship! And, believe it or not, this living, loving, powerful nugget of humanity has much in common with the nugget of the Holy Trinity.

We are celebrating moments when co-creation is manifested. We can ask about two dogs that are barking with each other. Do they really create anything together? I think not. But that makes it more important to ask about the uniqueness of human relationship. We want to ask what is really going on in the field of co-dialogue that even allows such things to happen.

What makes it work? We have attended closely to the co-statements, as each one is significant for deepening the interaction in which it occurred. Now we can look beyond that and observe other properties that are important.

We will consider four ways to understand the co-statement.

1. The co-statement is an interpersonal event of great meaning and power. This leads to the inversion of personal roles from speaker to listener.
2. It occurs in a field of rhetorical structures, such as noted above: inversions of role, and inversions of element and context. This second kind of inversion is described below.

3. Its occurrence is an event subject to scientific exploration;
4. Its occurrence leads beyond science to deeper understandings of human love and communication, human history, wisdom, and spiritual literature.

We have explored Diane's co-statement more deeply than the others. For that reason, the following considerations will be most clearly connected to Diane, though these properties are essentially the same for all co-statements. The most important significance of our study lies in what it may suggest about how we humans may more often dialogue with each other in beneficial ways—and recognize and grow from those benefits.

The first property to observe in this field is the interpersonal one. It is rather easy to see. The partners proceed with continual shifts in their role. The person in the role of speaker becomes listener as the listener becomes speaker. These are spontaneous shifts, and they appear to occur naturally and effortlessly. Continual shifts in role means continual shifts in perspective, which will naturally lead to changes in meaning. Bob's initial perspective seen in the light of Jane's response becomes a new perspective, and so on.

The second property occurs with a different kind of shift. We note that every statement has some effect on the meaning-flow. Usually it is a small effect. But with a co-statement, this effect can be quite large, so that many new topics are spontaneously brought up. When the co-statement first is spoken, it functions as an element in the mind of the speaker, and then of the listener. Initially it has little effect on the meaning-flow. But as its immense meanings are gradually recognized and absorbed by the partners, they are led to consider previously unexplored events and topics and feelings. So the field of meanings shifts and becomes greatly enlarged. That field comes to include many more events and feelings that had not been accessible in their dialogue. So we can say that the co-statement no longer is limited to functioning as an element. Instead, it functions as a context, and organizes those previously un-attended meanings. That produces sharing of yet more meanings and connections. The co-statement is the primary trigger for this inversion of function, this change in the dialogue's meaning-flow. For Diane, this new material includes much about her history of anger in relationships, and feeling important in that context.

These co-statements are not simply exchanges of information. In the larger frame, they are relational events which occur around an exchange of information. The information in the co-statement includes material from each partner. Each partner is changed by hearing the co-statement. Their relationship is deepened, and the topics that more or less spontaneously come up in the subsequent dialogue are thus also broadened and deepened. Each of the partners is given impetus to continue interacting on a deep level of meanings. Diane has given us a wonderful example of this kind of communication and its power, although she did not know that she was doing so. We can see that the occurrence of her co-statement will immediately draw attention to events in her life in which anger was a big problem. And there will be questions about what events have occurred that included her feeling important. Thus, we say, as above, that her co-statement's function inverts from that of an element to that of a context, which organizes the significance of the new material.

Third is the matter of hierarchy. As we have noted, there are two partners, a speaker and a listener. Being speaker carries a certain power in the dialogue, which the listener does not have. Thus there is a hierarchy. But that hierarchy is far from the usual type of hierarchy. This one is not permanent. It inverts spontaneously and often.

THE SCIENTIFIC/DESCRIPTIVE METHOD

The fourth way is through a scientific/descriptive method. What questions could we ask of science about this? In the first place, how did Diane's co-statement come to exist? And how did it come to affect her and me and our relationship—and also to affect you? Science would probably begin by noticing the sequence of necessary steps in the operation of a dialogue.

We will review several of those steps. We will use two fictional people, Bob and Jane, who are assumed to be already in the middle of an optimal dialogue. Bob is the client and Jane is the therapist. I use names of different genders only for ease of pronoun reference.

Anything that is said implying Bob's value as a person will be equally applicable to Jane's value as a person, and vice versa. They are equivalent in value, dignity, rights, importance, power to influence the course of the dialogue, and every other way, except their life experiences and perhaps psychological agility. One way in which you can interpret this usage is to convert every mention of "Bob" into "the patient"; and "Jane" into "the therapist." As we begin observing, Bob is speaker and Jane is listener. I have put Jane initially in the position of listening and being affected, which is the more necessary, difficult, and elusive function.

Their minds must do many things in order to carry on a dialogue, especially a dialogue that will bring them together in ways that expand their meanings and mutual understandings, and are beneficial to both of them. Here are some of those steps.

1. Automatic construction of co-statement:
   Each of them must gather pieces of information from his/her life experiences. These pieces will already be in some mental context. Bob constructs a statement. But this is not just any old statement. It is not like a dream or a monologue. It is also not like a command or a demand. It is automatically constructed so that it will elicit response from Jane.
2. New unexpected meanings:
   Bob's statement will include references to previous input from both himself and Jane. That is, it may be a co-statement. When it occurs, it will lead to a radical opening and deepening of new, unexpected topics in their subsequent dialogue, and a greater degree of soul-meeting between them. The relationship itself also will receive deeper organization. This has been described in chapter 2.
3. Healing through meeting:
   The sum of all this is that the partners engage in "healing through meeting." This consists in going further in mutuality so that healing occurs. That is a benefit for both Bob and Jane. It is a wonderful quality of us humans, that such an exchange is possible, and even beneficial.
4. Moving on to the products of this sequence:

Science might now look beyond this sequence, and turn its attention to the products of the sequence. That is, we ask "What does this sequence lead to?" The most prominent "product" is of course the co-statement. We see a single unexpectable statement that surprises us, as it somehow includes and affects both partners. It is active. It functions to produce beneficial changes in both partners. And we see that it has emerged from this very complex system which involves two persons, each of whom is already very complex (as every person is).

5. We can link better with science by using established scientific terminology. Thus, we use the technical term "complex system." What does this mean? We can best explain this with something that is not a complex system: a mechanical clock. The clock is a machine. Its parts interact in a way that is always completely predictable. They function in an orderly and unchangeable way. Each part interacts only with the one that comes before it and the one that comes after it. Thus, there is an order to them, a kind of line of action, so the interaction is called "linear."

6. A complex system is unpredictable:
In contrast, the term "complex system" is used to describe a collection of parts that interact with each other in ways that are *not* linear. A human mind is such a system. It has a lot of parts, a lot of thoughts, and a lot of interactions among them. Any person's sequence of thoughts is often very unpredictable. A patient's response to the therapist may be quite surprising, as was Diane's co-statement. Any co-statement will lead the partners to access a lot of new, unanticipated meanings. So we can say not only that the mind is a non-linear system, but also that it is quite complex.

7. A new science:
Fortunately, there is a new science, relatively unknown, that studies these things. We can call it complex systems theory, or general systems theory. It came to prominence in the mid-twentieth century, especially in the work of Von Bertalanffy.[2]

---

2. Bertalanffy, *General Systems Theory*, 32.

It is known especially in psychology. It is this science that gives us the claim, above, that certain things that we know about any relationship are very likely to also be found in every relationship. This includes each entity's allowing mutual affecting, giving and receiving, shifts in role, and shifts in the effect of any given piece of "influence" as it is shared. And there is mutual benefit from the interaction.

This new science will be greatly challenged to explain the function of even one person alone. Each person is extremely complex. But further than that, we are studying two such extremely complex systems that are interacting with each other and affecting each other in ways that converge constructively. Not only is each partner complex, but the interaction between them is far even more complex. This complex system theory will no doubt attempt to explain how it is possible for a (mere) dialogue to *bring about new levels of integration in each partner, and also in their relationship, with mutual benefit for both of them.*

The real scientific questions, then, include these: "How is it even possible that such real ongoing 'soul-to-soul' relationship and mutual affecting of each other can occur between humans?" "What kind of communicational 'laws' must they obey?" "What does this teach us about human consciousness, and especially about shared human consciousness?" And, "How can this kind of ongoing beneficial closeness be made more accessible to more people?"

These questions address not only scientific dimensions, but also major humanistic dimensions that we have seen in co-dialogues. And we have seen certain communicational events which can be shared with other humans. Thus, we have at least two sources for hope in making this beneficial closeness accessible to more people: the scientific/psychological and the humanistic. And we see that here in this very field, these two often disparate influences converge and become unified in the co-dialogue. We study the fact that the scientific "mechanical" linear properties of the field can be thought of as summed in our description, and those sums are recognized as humanistic properties such as mutuality and grace. For example, continual overt events of responding eventually add up to recognition of the humanistic quality of responsiveness. Continual events of receiving benefit with each other eventually add up to recognition of the humanistic quality of mutuality.

There are much broader fields that also deal with the "spiritual" interactions between such very complex entities. These include the field of teacher plus student, and of master plus disciple. Such fields also include theology and spirituality, and even philosophical anthropology, as is said of Martin Buber. These may be said to offer wisdom.

But often these fields offer statements that are perceived as abstract commands, not arising from a relationship, but rather from a monad. The superior—the teacher or master, gives a command to the inferior—the student or disciple. Many of these statements command us to love one another, or to obey "wisdom." They seem to come to us from a single voice, a monadic voice. We can perhaps imagine brain modules that could be activated by such monadic teachings, through the primal command: THOU SHALT NOT!

Probably, there are in addition brain modules and mind modules that are activated not by a monadic command, but by an image of being in a mutual relationship. Or by an image that is carried by a co-statement. Can this be an implicit form of love? One very prominent image comes to us from Jesus' commandment: "Love one another as I have loved you!" To paraphrase, consider it this way: "Re-create with each other the same kind of mutuality that you have had with me."

Can brain modules for such mutuality be activated also by other scriptural teachings? Or by spiritual practices, such as confessing to one another? Or unburdening one another? Or by "I-thou" relations? Or by being in therapeutic dialogue? In these co-statements, we have invitation to such imaginings. They carry mutuality, but more specifically they also carry instructions for how to perform mutuality in their particular case. With Diane, we consider both partners as drawn into images of oppositeness—here, of combining both anger and importance, and integrating of those two dimensions. In doing so, they actualize love.

Diane's co-statement, and the others that I have presented, are not just ideas about love, or commands that we ought to love one another. Rather, we "overhear" her co-statement. It becomes for us not a command (that might trigger resistance), but an *indirect invitation* to imagine the mutuality that is already portrayed in the co-statement, and then perhaps to actualize such mutuality with one of our significant others. In the sense of Diane, that would mean to integrate a conflict between anger and importance. One might ask a question of the significant other: "When you are so angry with me, do you really want to destroy my importance to you?" And such integrating is of course closely related to love.

We note that each of the other co-statements also invites its own particular kind of mutuality. Carol's invites openness to an unexpected hopeful message; Emily's invites resolution of distrust and rejection; Frances's invites attention to the terrible conflict between body and mind that is suffered by many who have been abused. Roland made a kind of accusation, and then healed it; Thomas metacommunicated positively about our conversation.

Let me propose a thought experiment: Imagine your favorite bulletin board where wisdom quotes are set out. I dare say that all the wisdom that you have ever seen on wisdom boards has come to you as monadic wisdom: the self-contained sage makes a pronouncement, a command, an "ought to love . . ." But it is not thereby automatically an inducement, or an invitation, or a seed, for a loving relationship. Since it comes as a command, it may stir resistance or defiance rather than loving relationship.

Albert, another patient, after many months of therapy, made a wonderful discovery. "I realized that a real man can be just like me!" Consider for instance that Albert's statement is put on a wisdom board. It has an inviting quality, as if to say "You, too, can try on this view." But if his statement were to be paraphrased into the form of traditional wisdom statements, it would say: "You should realize that a real man can be just like you." That form, however, has a "command" quality that could easily evoke resistance rather than joining.

In contrast, Diane's co-statement is dyadic. It is simultaneously both first person and second person. It does explicitly allude to our relationship. Perhaps you can imagine her co-statement of *dyadic wisdom* inscribed on such a board. It would invite people to *imagine* this particular pairing of modes of both anger and importance, and perhaps to apply it to their own life experience. Then it would function not as an injunction for compliance, but rather as an invitation, through a living example. You could even survey people's responses and find out whether anyone found this better than the monadic advice, as a way to enable him/her to be in beneficial relationship with another.

A fifth dimension of how the field works is in the actual change in meanings. We have noted above that the invertings of roles produces changes in perspective, which predispose to changes in meanings. Another dimension is "double description." When our mind receives two different descriptions of some entity, there may be a bonus. That is, a third entity may emerge. This is easily notable with our visual system. Each eye sees the world from a slightly different direction, so the images that it sends to the brain are different. Our brain synthesizes the two discrepant images into one image. But along with that, it creates the bonus of depth vision. As the dialogue progresses, both Bob and Jane get multiple implied descriptions of their selves. From that, the field is given the bonus of depth of identity in each of them.

We have noted also that the co-statement spontaneously "emerges" into the field. Its form is not at all predictable. Yet it brings many immediate connections to new material, and becomes an anchor for further changes in meanings.

In these explorations, we have often seen that a unification takes place between two diverse entities. An element in the dialogue can become united with its context, so as to generate much clearer meaning for both the element and the context. The therapist, coherent in him/her self, can become united with his/her words and actions, and be made one with them in full presence. And the two partners can become united into a relationship. This kind of unifying into oneness will be prominent in chapter 6, "A pointer toward the Trinity," and chapter 7, "Benefiting with each other in the image of the Trinity."

Chapter 5

On Relationship Itself

Now we turn to the most important human dimension of our work here so far: relationship itself, with some abstractions about it. To come closer to an understanding of relationship, we have asked this question: What kind of world must exist in order to make it possible for this epitome of interaction, a co-statement, to occur? And what kind of world must exist to allow for the occurrence of true relationship and co-created dialogue and exchanging of benefits with each other?[1] We are proclaiming a world-view within which such phenomena do exist, and in which their implications can make sense and be harvested for wisdom about living well with each other.

Good relationship is manifested when each partner both gives and receives meanings with the other, and they allow themselves to be changed by each other in their interaction. Here, our

---

1. In answer to this question, I offer a reminder of the earlier quote from Teilhard: "Properly observed, even if only in one spot, a phenomenon necessarily has an omnipresent value and roots by reason of the fundamental unity of the world. . . . [We are given] to discover the universal hidden beneath the exceptional" (*Phenomenon*, 55–56). And here, building upon his work, we are able to go further than he did in mining the meanings of true interpersonal relationship and mutual exchange of benefits.

explorations have been focused on a particular peak of such giving and receiving, which I have called the co-statement. When a co-statement occurs, it represents the best working of the interaction. Every co-statement creates a new level of connection between the partners, and thus enhances the interaction between them. It has major effects in broadening the topics in the meaning-flow in the ongoing dialogue. That enhanced meaning-flow will further deepen the interaction, so that their interaction becomes worthy to be called relationship.

Up until now, our considerations of interaction and relationship have been mostly secular. I have been separating secular formulations from religious ones, so as to look for their similarities—and maybe someday their unification! More about this as we go on. Although we have hinted at the role of "spirit," we have done so in a way that is mostly descriptive. We have not yet used the notion of spirit as related to the power of co-dialogue. But now we can speak of this spirit-power which includes the givings and receivings, the mutuality and grace, the emerging of purpose and future in both partners, and the involvement of the divine in the relationship.

The field of relationship manifests itself in qualities that sparkle like a diamond, and are ineffable like the divine. In our descriptions, we no sooner get a glimpse of some sparkle of relational glory than a shift occurs, and a different glory comes into view. What are some of these glories? To name a few, we can mention authenticity and soul-speak and mutuality and personhood as it is being exchanged. The new economy of personhood is given and received in charmed loops of continual deepening. (A charmed loop is the opposite of a vicious cycle. It is charmed because it is the embodiment of positive feedback in the cybernetic sense. It is not merely positive in "saying nice things" to someone, but rather, it is positive in that it produces more and more increase in itself.)

Thus, the field hosts mystery. It first reveals and then shifts to conceal. It combines the un-knowable with the knowable, the unexpectable with the expectable. We will find that it is impossible to be completely coherent in praising or even describing such glory.

However, when a co-statement occurs, its occurrence constitutes praise and glory of the relationship itself, and of the field.

In chapter 7, we will move on to use what we are discovering about such relationship, as we explore some of what has been imputed to divine relationships. Von Bertalanffy offers us good reason to expect that *any* relationship will have important features in common with every other relationship, of any size or complexity. The partners offer their selfs to each other, both as givers of self and as receivers of self, as self-hood is exchanged in words, and the partners generate WE-hood. The partners affect and are affected by each other again and again. We will ask how such interactions may also be joined by divine relationship.

In that chapter, we will go even further, to consider how divine relationships may come rather directly into our human lives. The divine beings, Father, Son, and Holy Spirit, distribute their self to us and they enjoy being magnified by our responsive resonating with them as they do so. They can infuse us; they joy in helping us fulfill our approach to ideal giving and receiving of love among each other.

"THE QUICKENING"

Here is a story from Martin Buber[2] that combines the human with the divine. Buber and others have said that when you and I talk, there is spirit. It is not that spirit is in me, or in you; rather, spirit is *between* us, *among* us (*zwischen*). In his work of collecting Hasidic tales, Buber[3] reports a tale which proclaims this point very well. It is called "The Quickening."

> They asked Rabbi Pinhas: "Why is it, that a person who sees his friend after an interval of more than twelve months, says the blessing 'Who quickenest the dead'?"
>
> He answered: "Every human being has a light in Heaven. When two meet, the lights fuse, and a new light shines out of them. This is called a begetting, and the new

2. Buber, *I and Thou*, 39.
3. Buber, *Hasidism*, 127.

light is an angel. This angel, however, cannot live longer than twelve months, unless those two beings meet on earth again before the time is up. But if they meet after the twelve months have passed, they can quicken the angel again for a time. That is why they say that blessing."[4]

The phrase "who quickenest the dead" refers not only to one friend's being quickened by the other, but also to the inversion of that. That is, each individual is quickening the other. Not only the individuals, but also their relationship itself is quickened. So "a new light" shines out of them. And indeed, they go on to experience that new life in their renewed relationship.

DIMENSIONS OF RELATIONSHIP

The cornerstone of relationship in co-dialogue is that each of the partners is willing and able to let their self be affected, even "quickened," by giving and receiving with the other. These two processes differ from each other. Giving is a form of revealing oneself with the anticipation of affecting the partner; receiving is a form of opening to let oneself be affected. Both of these functions require radical openness. The partners evoke mutual beneficial changes in each other, and this can even represent a form of love. In mutuality, each partner may say: I am loved not just by you, but also by noticing myself-responding-to-your-love.

CONTENTS OF MUTUALITY: WINDOW AND MIRROR

Let us consider the content of such mutuality. Can we name some of the sparkles? Let us start with windows and mirrors. Bob reveals some part of his history and feelings. We can name this a window function: he allows Jane to look through the "window" into himself. But he may do so without a corresponding mirror function. That is, he may not have given full consent to her looking in and seeing him as he is, in ways that he may not have recognized. Instead, he may

---

4. Buber, *Hasidism*, 127.

be reporting facts, letting Jane know those facts, but not including his own sense of participating in the revealing of those facts. He reports himself as a sort of duty. He is unable to let himself be mirrored by his own statements.

Also, he may speak only from his mirror, so that he may appear to be concealing himself, locked into reflecting on himself, and unable to let himself be open to effects from Jane. This would echo Carol, and her depressive inability to let herself be given hope.

In the best cases, Bob becomes able to speak simultaneously as both window and mirror. When that happens, we experience him as authentic. We can say that he gives some of his self-hood to Jane. In his authenticity, he may make a statement that includes a high degree of both window and mirror, which Jane may experience as "soul-speak." Through her good listening, she is able to recognize it as coming to her *from his soul*. She will of course be edified that she has recognized that. She will receive his soul-speak as a gift, and then she and he will be together in the realm of mutuality.

Emergence of Personhood:

Going further, we may expect to see loveliness in both of them. The field will be full with their mutual giving and receiving of deep meaning and love. This is a kind of saturation. We may name it personhood. Personhood is that quality of being in relationship that recognizes that the state of being a full person comes through relating with other persons. The partners give it to each other by speaking from their souls—and they receive it from each other by listening from their souls.

Then we will notice a great mystery. When soul-speak is given, the giver is blessed, and also the one who recognizes it is blessed. This is one way to constitute personhood. When such personhood is given, the receiver is blessed, as well as the giver. There is a new economy: no longer a zero-sum economy, as with giving beans and then having fewer of them; but rather, a charmed loop of interaction through which more and more blessings emerge.

At this point, we may begin to see hints of spirit. Spirit is an insideness-outsideness operator. It facilitates these charmed loops of meaning and love that move from inside one partner, outside into the field, and then to the inside of the other partner. In addition, spirit is itself further amplified in the operation of these loops that it has already initiated and facilitated.

The Content of What is Given and Received: I AM!:

When Bob gives some of his self from his mirror-soul, it is as if he is following the God of Moses, announcing: "I AM!" Jane has two possible responses to his announcement: competition or affirmation. Jane may experience Bob's announcement as something of a challenge, as if he were saying: "I AM and therefore you are not. My being supersedes yours. You are not important." Here we hear an echo of Diane. In response to this perceived challenge, Jane may counter Bob and say: "Oh! Then I assert that I AM too!" Indeed, Diane did just that, as she processed her perception that I was mad with her. She proclaimed her own existence and importance by making her co-statement.

In contrast, Jane may try a two-step response. She may affirm Bob's announcement by responding, in effect: "Yes. You ARE. I accept the fact that you exist." This would affirm Bob's existence and his importance. In this imaginary dialogue, Jane may later go to the next stage of relationship, by reasoning as follows: "Since you ARE, and since I now see that I have a self with which to receive and appreciate your announcement of your existence, I can say: 'Oh! I AM too.'" Thus, she experiences her own self-hood as a gift from Bob. In co-dialogue, both partners may become able to affirm both of these dimensions of their existences vis-a-vis each other. When they have come to that mutual affirmation of each other, then the field is set for the spontaneous emergence of WE-hood: their awareness of being in full relationship.

Let me try to summarize this sequence. To give personhood to someone means that I become aware that I am flowing from my own deep sense of wholeness and love (from my mirror), and thus

I am able to treat that person in a way that *calls forth* his/her own deep sense of wholeness and loveliness and personhood, and our connection *in* those qualities: *their shareability* for both of us. We become WE. And the sharing of that loveliness and personhood in WE is a "charmed loop" that makes those qualities grow for both of us! We can speak of giving and receiving loveliness and personhood! And we can notice the mystery residing in and arising from that sharing. And further, we can claim that the relationship itself, the WE, the mutuality, the sharing of personhood, the mystery—all of these are host to spirit!

(We wish to be careful, at this stage, about using words like "mystery" and "spirit." The term "mystery" will be used to refer to a person or a phenomenon or a context that cannot be known completely, and yet has "being" and is active among us. The term "spirit" is more difficult, because there are so many different interpretations of it. Spirit clearly is a mystery, but it is much more than that. We may speak of a human spirit, and also of a divine Spirit. A spirit may be hosted by a mystery. It is difficult to imagine a spirit that could be known apart from some mystery. Yet in the field of co-dialogue, we clearly do have mystery, which resides in complexity and surprise. What could be added to that mystery to further justify our saying that it hosted spirit? Maybe the proper distinction is that spirit is active in relationships, while mystery, expected to be irrational, is a passive context for spirit.)

Word-based Relationship and Its Contagion:

Probably for all of human history, great verbal relationship with reciprocation has existed in the mystery of mutuality. But until recently, it has rarely been mentioned as a subject in itself, except in vague admonitions to love one another. The advent of psychotherapy has given us much more precise ways of understanding real relationship, and of accomplishing it. We have claimed that moments of good verbal relationship can even be "contagious." They can be transmitted to others. The co-statement functions as a fruit, and also as a seed: it "seeds" a predisposition toward mutuality among certain listeners.

Beyond these human relationships, we can also turn to the divine, and note that such ideal relationship has been imputed to occur in the Trinity, and is contagious—transmittable to us—in our human relationships. More about that in chapter 7.

COUNTER-EXAMPLES

For clarity, let us consider some counter-examples, in which attention to relationship is impaired. DeQuincey has said that our current philosophy of relationship is as yet very poorly developed. He described three different modes of the philosophy of consciousness.

> Standard third person inquiry (about "it") leads to a science of external bodies, first person inquiry (about "I") to a science of the mind, while second person engagement (about "you") leads to a *communal science of the heart*. Whereas the ultimate ideal of objective knowledge is control, and the ultimate ideal of subjective knowledge is peace, the ultimate ideal of intersubjective knowledge is relationship—and, dare I say it, love![5]

The history of our race and our theologies is full of examples of individuals, mostly rulers, who function with unilateral power. They treat other persons as objects to be controlled. That is, they assume the power to affect without being affected. Many theologies postulate a god who is like that: "impassible," unable and perhaps unwilling to suffer or to be affected at all. And many notions about ideal politicians suggest political rule which exercises unilateral power. According to Mesle, such unilateral power "inherently inhibits the growth of value in human experience."[6] He quotes Whitehead: "We must reject those images . . . which falsely elevate success in the pecking order to this supreme image of ideal personhood." In contrast, the ability of both partners to affect and be affected is

---

5. De Quincey, *Radical Knowing*, 180.
6. Mesle, "Aesthetic Value and Relational Power."

"relational power," the essential foundation for the growth of value in human experience.

The increased attention to relationship in our time may help us to notice this contrast: in the past, our own culture's attention to relationship has been inhibited, and has been very slow to come. One example arises from psychoanalysis, which has sometimes insisted that the analyst should not be affected by what happens between him/her and the patient. This is an echo of the "oriental potentate," who is assumed to have so much power that he doesn't need any response from his subjects. Some business people seem to partake of the same illusion. Transferring this phenomenon to religion, we ask: do we feel attracted to believing in a god whose mercy and compassion are given without affecting that god? A god who has that power to affect without being affected?

Examples of Inhibition in Humanistic Spheres:

But this inhibition has been apparent in humanistic spheres as well. Here are three examples, where the explicit mention of reciprocating giving and receiving of beneficial statements—such as in interpersonal love—could have been expected, but did not occur:

Example 1: A Proposed Vision of Human Nature is Found in Kaufman:

> Imbedded in all psychological theories . . . is an ideology about the nature of human beings and the cosmos. That ideology consists of a vision of optimal development; a vision of the interface between human beings and the universe; a vision of the interaction between psyche and soma, mind and body, consciousness and brain; a vision of what is good and what is bad . . .[7]

Can you think of any important dimension of psychology that is not represented in this statement? What else could conceivably

---

7. Kaufman, *Shame*.

be added to such ideals? From our perspective here, it is obvious. Kaufman might have added *a vision of the interaction between one human and another human*—that field of interaction and relationship that is so crucial for the survival of our race.

Example 2: Mother Already Knows:

Therapist: "Did you tell your mother that you feel more urgent about getting together?"
Patient: "No, because she already knows it."
Therapist: "Yes. But that is a very different thing. Believing that she already knows it, without any real shared or shareable statements about it, is quite different from actually saying it to her."

This little snippet of dialogue illustrates an insufficiency of relationship, and the unused relational power of spoken word. There is a large difference between whether something is "true" within one's own thought vs. whether it is externalized to someone outside oneself. The usefulness of such externalization lies in the fact that it can lead to the possibility of improved relationship.

Example 3: Simpler Living, Compassionate Life:

Here is a quote from Schut:

> Love all of God's creation, the whole of it and every grain of sand. Love every leaf, every ray of God's light! Love the animals, love the plants, love everything. If you love everything, you will perceive the divine mystery in things. And once you have perceived it, you will begin to comprehend it ceaselessly, more and more every day. And you will at last come to love the whole world with an abiding, universal love.[8]

This is a beautiful quote, and a worthy ideal, featuring our relationships with "all of God's creation." *Simpler Living* attributes it

---

8. Schut, *Simpler Living*, 216.

to Dostoyevsky, in *The Brothers Karamazov*.[9] But in Dostoyevsky's original version, this passage is actually *preceded* by Dostoyevsky's reference to a far more important love: that between one human and another:

> Brothers, do not be afraid of men's sin, love man also in his sin, for this likeness of God's love is the height of love on earth.

Thus, "Simpler Living" has left out the very statement that describes the "nitty-gritty" of the love that their quote otherwise advocates.

THE NITTY-GRITTY OF RELATIONSHIP ENERGY

What can we say here about that "nitty-gritty"? One person gives personhood to another person *in his/her sin,* and energy of relationship is noted. Such energy can produce changes. Here we are speaking of changes toward more complex mutuality and more intense grace. The nature of personhood is such that the act of giving oneself produces more energy not only in the receiver, but in the giver as well. Thus, we have a new economy, as above. There come to be more changes and more benefits. This property of giving and receiving and generating new energy and new personhood is a further suggestion that the term "spirit" would be fitting.

The Unification of the Two Partners Into Relationship:

The system that encompasses the two somehow comes to have more total energy. As the partners interact, and as they exert effects upon one another, and as we recognize them as unified into a developing relationship, we will be able to see more clearly that some energy or power is present.

It is still impossible to say whether that power is a new entity that is generated in and by the dialogue; or whether the power pre-exists the dialogue and energizes it, and even is magnified by it. In either case, we may speak of the power as "spirit." It is a

---

9. Dostoyevsky, *Brothers Karamazov*, 318–19.

simultaneous affirmation of both listener and speaker, and it thus affirms relationship between them. It super-saturates their field with mutuality and love. It is able to both precede and follow the meanings and effects, linking them with the past and future of both partners and of their sharing in relationship. Consider the old hymn "Crown Him with Many Crowns."[10] It includes the line: "Fruit of the mystic rose and of that rose the stem"; thus it expresses such joined following and preceding.

Equality of Partners?:

Sometimes, it is asserted that in a good enough relationship, the two partners must be considered to be equal. It can certainly be said that they are equal in importance of presence, since the dialogue could not take place if either of them were not present. And if we had some way to make a summation of the meaning-contributions of each, we might be able to assert that these are equal in importance to the ongoing co-dialogue.

But actually, the attention to claims of equality serves to hide the dynamic processes of the interaction. At any given moment, one partner (say, Bob) is speaking, while the other (Jane) is not. Bob's speaking partakes of certain processes: neurological, psychological, social; while Jane's listening partakes of very different facets of the same neurological, psychological, social processes.

At such a moment, the two are not "equal" in the usual sense; rather, they are complementary. At a subsequent moment, their roles invert, and the neurological and psychological and social dimensions also invert. Bob becomes silent; Jane speaks, and Bob listens. With each inversion, the complementarity continues. Obviously, relationship requires both complements.

Bob is subject, and he takes Jane as his object. Is this domination? Some commentators have portrayed post-modernism as insisting that competition for such domination is universal in dialogue, and there is no escaping it. Yet we see that in co-dialogue, Bob's "domination" is exercised with Bob's full expectation that he will "submit" it

---

10 *ELW*, #855.

to Jane, voluntarily and spontaneously. Bob becomes willing and able to give up his position of quasi-dominance, and surrender that position to Jane, and become himself an object of Jane's subjectivity. Then she becomes "dominant" and Bob "submits" to her statements. As we have seen, the roles invert frequently and naturally. The alternation of roles occurs naturally, as naturally as inhaling then exhaling, and flexing then extending a muscle. This naturalness belies the notion that dialogue is always a competition for dominance.

THE TENDENCY TO REPAIR THE FIELD

The nature of the field of co-dialogue includes the tendency of either partner to repair the field whenever a disturbance occurs, such as attempts to dominate, or to withdraw; or through an error by the therapist. The case of Roland above, about prostitution and my mistake of therapeutic technique, shows that the patient may be the one who initiates a repair of the field. The therapist, upon recognizing that his/her sense of connectedness is waning, may initiate a repair. A useful statement is: "Right now, I feel that I am not understanding you very well. Let me take a break and let's both listen for what's going on." A brief trip to get a cup of coffee often brings a new insight for healing the listening.

Some may feel that whatever occurs between the partners in the relationship is done not by the statements themselves, but by the persons. Indeed, our language is ambiguous. We may sometimes speak of what an effect Roland had on the field; but we may equally well speak of what an effect his statement had on it. "When he said that, I felt . . ."

NEW LEVELS OF MENTAL ABILITY; NEW TYPES OF RELATIONSHIP

By now you may have realized that these processes are very similar to the interactional processes which have characterized all evolution of life. New levels of organization of life have emerged, easily seen in the study of biological evolution. New levels of mental ability have also emerged for homo sapiens as a whole. And in each person's development, new levels occur again and again for him/her, as we see, for example, in Erikson's[11] stages of psychosocial development.

And new types of relationship have occurred throughout our evolution. We have been contextualized in family and tribes; myth tellers and listeners; web friendships and chat rooms; psychotherapy relationships of many kinds, and recognition of I-thou relationships. Also relationships with pastors, teachers, rabbis, shamans, and interest groups. In our study of co-dialogue, we can now recognize and harvest the fact that new levels of deepening relationship occur, both in the moments of our relationships, and in the memories of them.

A co-statement has the effect of simultaneously contextualizing both partners and thus producing WE (or expanding the degree of WE). The co-statement's very occurrence is evidence of WE-hood, including past, present, and future WE. A co-statement is a stimulus to both Jane and Bob. When it occurs, both of them are responding to the same stimulus.

My friend James (not his real name) is an alcoholic. He believes deeply in AA and the Twelve Steps. He likes to talk about them. On one occasion, he recited the powerful story of Bill W. and his experiences in starting AA, especially with "Dr. Bob." James has owned that story, and so it has become his own story, which he shared with me with great warmth. We both shed tears as we joined in appreciation of the story. It has become a touchstone for our love for each other, and our sharing many other meanings with each other. As he long ago received Bill W.'s story, it has become his story, and he also recognizes it as God's story; and as he tells it to me, it becomes our story—mine as well as his and God's.

Just hearing such a story of a very good relationship may generate a sense of being drawn into it. This may also occur with other great stories, great literature and poetry. War-time stories of heroism can function in that way. Rabbinical stories like those attributed to the Baal Shem Tov and many others can also function in that way. And the stories of Jesus and his relationships with his disciples

---

11. Erikson, *Childhood*, 247–74.

can powerfully change us as we allow ourselves to be drawn into their relationships. Thus I claim that these stories of co-statements also have power to go forth and change you who are reading and listening to these stories, you who may even pass them on to others. Be blessed in WE-hood.[12]

---

12. Teilhard has a phrase that points strongly in this direction. He says that the cyclone of evolution, now on the social scale, is "driving us together into a contact which tends to perfect each one of us by linking him organically to each and all of his neighbors" (*Phenomenon*, 305). This offers a grand vision of WE-hood.

Chapter 6

"Tum Tose" Points Toward the Trinity

My mother often mentioned this little story from my childhood. It illustrates a spirit of connection and love between me and my mother and my father. She called it "Tum Tose" (that is, "Come Close"). It points toward the Trinity, because it presents a triad of persons loving each other in a way that is generating more and more love among them all—more than enough for each of them, and more than enough to overflow to bless others, and indeed to bless you as you read it. We will join O'Donnell, who writes about von Balthasar and his powerful assertion: "Being is love. Being is the trinitarian love of the Father and the Son in the Holy Spirit."[1] Then we can claim another powerful assertion: the Persons of the Holy Trinity are engaged in eternal utterly complete giving and receiving of love *and being* among all Three of them.

Since it is such a powerful assertion, we can parse it further. We can say that each of them is engaged in utterly complete giving,

---

1. O'Donnell, *Hans Urs von Balthasar*, 6–7. O'Donnell shows, in a very fullsome way, Balthasar's beliefs and statements about the Trinity. In many ways, our concrete examples here in WE-hood actualize many of Balthasar's abstract claims about relationships, both human and divine and human-divine (139–44).

to the point of emptying; and then utterly complete receiving, to the point of being full to overflowing.

This giving and receiving is in some sense parallel to the human triad of love that I present below, in Tum Tose, though the Trinity is of course far more sublime.

(I choose to speak in these Christian terms because I am much more familiar with them. If any of you find that any other religion or philosophy speaks *operationally* to these issues of persons joining in mutuality and grace and relationship, I would be very grateful to hear from you.)

Our ways of describing ideal divine relationships will include methods and content that are different from the ways we have already found to describe ideal human relationships. That is unavoidable, since we have immediate knowledge of the human dimensions, but not of the divine dimensions. But the proceedings of the two types of relationship are taken to be very similar: both of them generate mutuality and love and wisdom, and both operate in a positive feedback loop that generates more and more mutuality and love and wisdom. The human and the divine seen abstractly are very similar, though they differ greatly in magnitude and grandeur and power.

"TUM TOSE"

A little boy, barely able to talk, sees his parents standing together in an embrace. He senses their closeness, as it shines out from their love. The boy goes to them, and wraps his little arms around their legs, and says "Tum tose."

Since they of course know baby talk, they hear him to mean "come close." Though he cannot yet know it so clearly, he is saying: "The two of you, do keep on loving each other and drawing me into your loving closeness. Let me always be a part of your WE."

That event took place more than seventy years ago. Why would I be remembering it after so many years? The answer lies in this: I have come to realize that, in this piece of baby talk, I was naively expressing what turns out to be a deep truth about relationship. At our best we join and participate with each other, and actively bring out each other's love. This "double loving" or "triple loving" begets love that flows out from our WE toward many others.

For this kind of relational event, words fall far short. Yet we who know must speak. Each such moment is a womb in the desert, which begets love from hidden nurtures that wait to take form in new connections with each other: the seeds of seeking, and of finding.

We give, and receive, and grow, and do not know the words for what it is that we are giving and receiving and growing with. My mother and daddy did not know that I, in my naiveté, would speak into their embrace. Yet they heard me with joy, and spoke of it, even years later. I dare say that my little words amplified their love for each other, and at the same time brought them to deeper love and appreciation for me. Maybe even to greater gratitude for me.

Such words can be called words of life, as well as words of love. Is this a deep truth that needs a philosopher to unveil it? Or a psychiatrist? We who know must speak, and proclaim the occurrence of such events that bring together livingness, lovingness, and shared soul, as each person magnifies the love of the others.

My patients and I do not know which of us will speak the words that consummately express our WE! When one of us does so, our very togetherness invites me, and invites him or her, to further deepen, to feast on our words of life and love, to join in flowering more of it forever.

I have spent many years in a "practice" of relationships with both patients and friends. Being a slow learner about that sort of thing, I am just now realizing the power of the "tum tose" moment. It occurred long ago, but it is still occurring in my soul, resonating in my memory of Mother and Daddy, and seeding my notions about all relationship, all communion.

I am not naive any longer. I know too well that too many of us cannot remember moments of such closeness with our parents—or with anyone else. And yet we yearn for them "like a deer longs for the water brooks." We yearn for tenderness, love, connection—and the mutual affirmation that these carry.

Sometimes in our despair, we even deny ourselves the right to realize what would really help us, and we deflect the affirmations that we so much need. Anna was a patient who had suffered severe anxiety from much terrible abuse. One day, after many months of treatment, I suggested, as gently as I knew how, that she might someday experience peace. She cursed me.

It is into such a desert of deprivation that I am compelled to speak. We come together into dialogue, and co-create nurturance in new meanings and affirmations and togetherness. It is a fact that we sometimes can relieve the deprivation. Fast forward about two years. One day, Anna came to her session and proudly announced: "Doc, this morning, I had ten minutes of peace!"

Can we become able to do it more often and more effectively? Tum tose!

Let us shift our focus and take another look at what is really going on here. This "tum tose" episode, as a whole, shines with a light full of love. That love arises, of course, from the relationship among the three people involved. And I dare say that their love, as contained in this story of their love, is powerful enough to beget images of closeness in you, and perhaps to call in your own memories of such moments of love.

In the most immediate sense, this episode takes place on a purely human-human level. These three people constitute a very special nugget, a radiant nexus of giving and receiving love with each other with a high degree of warmth.

But in addition, we can intuit a "spirit" charming the interaction, magnifying the love among the three of us. We can then expect that such a spirit of charmed interaction will likely have some significance on a divine level too. There may be many such nuggets in godhead relations, though I know of only one. That one, most accessible to me as a Christian, is the Holy Trinity. Those trinitarian Three, too, are a very special and glorious nugget. As we noted above, they are said to be engaging in eternal utterly complete giving and receiving of love among them—and that is much like my parents and I did, though we were on a much less sublime level.

This parallel between the observable human-human level and the postulated divine level will be explored further as we go on. We will find that the Holy Trinity can actually become our friend, and love us by name. Thus we can invite them in their Unity to come and join us as we too become one in each loving relationship. The Trinity can deepen us and empower us in loving each other. Just as *the Three's* love for each other overflows onto us, they may lead us further in letting our human-become-divine love spill over to many others.

Chapter 7

Benefiting with Each Other in the Image of God as Trinity

"The grace of our Lord Jesus Christ, the love of God, and the fellowship of the Holy Spirit be with you all" (2 Cor 13:14 RSV).

EXPANDING OUR UNDERSTANDINGS OF RELATIONSHIP

With the great blessing of this beautiful benediction, which is clearly about fellowship in relationships, we are now ready to expand our understandings of our own relationships, and their possible connection with the divine. This benediction evokes the Trinity: the Son, the Father, and the Holy Spirit, and it can lead us to imagine their relationship with each other, with all of its love and sparkles and depths.

In chapter 5, I made a claim that the very occurrence of co-statements in our world leads us to infer certain things about basic realities of our world and our relationships in it. These realities include the facts that relational love exists in verbal interactions and that it can manifest as fruit and seed. And I asked how we can

Benefiting with Each Other in the Image of God as Trinity

harvest those inferences, and be led to wisdom about living well with each other.

Now we expand that question and ask about not only our human world, but also about the world of the divine. In this chapter, we will attend to certain parallels and convergences of the divine world with the human world, and consider how these convergences may bring deeper benefits and mutuality and wisdom to the partners, and also to others who learn about them.

This is even more important when we consider a statement that could be co-created between a human and God. Such a statement may be specially empowered to have beneficial effects on others. Such co-creation may have played a part even in some parts of the Bible and other inspired works. Consider Isaiah's prophecy that "his name shall be called Wonderful, Counselor, The mighty God, The Everlasting Father, The Prince of Peace" (Isa 9:6–7 KJV). Also see "chaplains" below.

Nouwen has quoted Rogers, who has written much more poetically about the human dimension of this:

> I have found that the very feeling which has seemed to me most private, most personal and hence most incomprehensible by others, has turned out to be an expression for which there is a resonance in many other people. It has led me to believe that what is most personal and unique in each one of us is probably the very element which would, if it were shared or expressed, speak most deeply to others.[1]

This quote from Rogers does not mention the divine. But here we can go further, and explore parallels between the human and the divine, especially the Holy Trinity. Like us humans in dialogue, those Three can be said to exist in WE-hood. Thus they too can say to each other: "You-I-You-I-OH!" as they are surprised to discover newer and newer depths of love and mutuality in their ongoing WE-hood, and in their various activities in the world. As we join their field of reciprocation and mutuality, as we join their WE, we

---

1. Nouwen, *Wounded Healer*, 74.

may become able to generate even more love and powerful meanings, and thus to benefit each other better in their image.

THE IMAGE OF GOD IN INDIVIDUALS AND IN RELATIONSHIPS

We are taught that God said: "Let us make man in our image, after our likeness . . . "So God created man in his own image, in the image of God created he him; male and female created he them" (Gen 1:26–28 KJV). And it is a very strong part of our tradition that God is *one*. So we are led to assume that "being created in the image of God" means that God created us as "one's"; that is, as individuals. This is a powerful notion for our prayer and meditation. But there is more.

As we have already hinted, we can go beyond our individuality, and ask about our relationships, our WE-hood. Then we will be in wonder that each relationship involving two (or more) such individual selves can be understood to be made in the image of God the Trinity. That is, made in the image of the Trinity as WE, as they are eternally utterly completely giving love with each other—*and with us humans;* and also utterly completely receiving love with each other—*and with us humans*. In this chapter, we will explore the recognition that *our* relationships—our human-human WE-nesses—have discernible and powerful parallels with the WE-ness that we impute to the Trinity. And we note that the one-ness of those Three does not occur as homogenization into complete sameness, but as harmonization into different living chords of divine relational love, a symphony of love. We hope to let this Trinity be a friend to us!

THE TRINITY IS A PARADOX: BOTH COSMIC AND PARTICULAR

We are entering sacred space. So please join me in this guided meditation, whether you substantially "believe" in the Trinity or not. We will contemplate these ideal spiritual relationships and be surprised at their parallels with the human-human relationships that we have been studying.

The Trinity comes to us as a paradox. On one hand, for a Christian, it is the magnificence of all creation. The Father is self-distributive, giving his very self-of-love in the grandeur of the entire cosmos; giving himself to Jesus the Christ in the grandeur of the Holy Spirit, and embodying the total sum of Christians' salvation history: Creation, Incarnation, and Pentecost, the occasion of the founding of the church as community.

On the other hand, this magnificence is also the particularity, the singularity, of events of God's self-distribution. God joys in giving himself. He comes to each of us as we are *individual*. Who could have imagined that the God of all creation would know your name, and come to be with you, Ralph? As you grow in the faith, you may come to moments of communion when you as an individual feel God's hug. The Spirit grabs you and says "You are mine. And I love you." The Trinity is itself a nugget of such love. The Three-in-One are like a diamond. They sparkle in ways that are delightful, especially as each sparkle is unique and unrepeatable in its beauty, while it is also being powerful in the ability to connect us with them through loving relationship. Both of these dimensions of Trinity coincide in our belief, mentioned above, that they are engaged in eternal utterly complete giving and receiving of love among the Three of them. Both the grandeur and the particularity are parts of such exchanges of love, where BEING itself arises. And love and being are communicated to us humans through their love.

We in Our Co-dialogue are Configured to Receive the Trinity:

Our human relationships of giving and receiving with each other in a two-some generate a human-level configuration that will be quite congruent to the Trinity in their Three-ness as they too give and receive with each other. Thus our relationship will be hospitable to receiving the WE-configuration of the Trinity. It should be relatively easy for us to receive their love and its interpersonal power for modeling our relationships after them. This will further our own giving and receiving in love. Thus, the source of our love in relationship would come not from *our* insides, or *our* will power or our intention; rather, our love comes as a gift from the Trinity, from their dance of generating love with each other and indwelling us with their co-created love.

Recognizing the Love They Offer to Our Relationships:

We are not looking for an ability for us, on our own power, to love the Trinity. Rather, we are looking for a way for us to recognize the love that is offered to us from them—and *then* return it to them. The Trinity in its/their one-ness-in-relationship is itself the origin and generator of divine love. It is already aimed at us, and it gives us the power to love one another. Compare this to the Tum Tose story. There, three human loves come together. Their coming together generates much more love, which will inspire and strengthen our relationships.

But far grander is the interactional love of the Holy Three, taken as an ideal entity. Their Three-ness-in-One-ness gives them unique power to *beget* love *in each other* and to give it to us. Theirs is an extremely powerful configuration of love among each other, and also they joy as they overflow in offering their love to us. We, in turn, may welcome their love into our relationships, and that may lead us to say this: "Not only is our individuality made in the image of God the One, but also our relationships are made in the image of the God the Three, God's "internal" relationships as Three-in-One.

As you read what follows, you will find many references to the Trinity. Together, these offer a kind of implicit definition of It/Them. Within their relationship, they are Three who are also simultaneously One. They are eternally engaged in the utterly complete giving and receiving of love with each other. That creates an immense divine mutuality within their One-ness, full of openness with each other. As above, they can be imagined to be continually saying to each other, "You-I-You-I-OH!" as they are continually surprised at getting to know each other more and more deeply. Their love is fruitful within them, as they give and receive more and more love. It also is fruitful for us, as it spills out into us, into our relationships. They are a dynamo for generating love recursively, in a charmed loop that is always growing in love, always magnifying their love, and always sending love to us. Indeed, their love can make our own relationships become such a dynamo. One definition of a "saint" is someone whose loving relationships are such a dynamo.

You will also note many uses of the phrase "giving and receiving." It is indeed a very important dynamic of love in all relationships. You will find this phrase usually as "giving and receiving love." But also, it will refer to giving and receiving information, meanings, personhood, and mutual benefit. At times, it must also be interpreted as giving completely, unto emptiness. And receiving completely into over-flowing. It is the principal dynamic of both human dialogue and intra-trinitarian dialogue. And we say that the very process of giving and receiving in these ways generates more and more such mutual benefit and love.

"Spirit" Talk is Mystery:

I have invited you to suspend any unbelief that you may have about such spirit, and/or about the Trinity, and consider all talk about spiritual things to be mystery, best spoken of in metaphors. Below, I will speak about some glimpses into the mystery. I will be using Christian thought, but I welcome anyone of any religion or of no religion to offer your thoughts about the role of spirit in human relationships.

(I will continue the convention of mostly using plural pronouns to refer to the Trinity, to avoid the awkward formula "It/Them": "it" for one-ness and "them" for three-ness. Also, I freely acknowledge the difficulties of referring to the divine with gender-based pronouns. I apologize for that, but I don't know any better way to speak of them.)

(Also, I will continue the convention of using the fictitious names Bob and Jane in these human relationships, with the same proviso that Bob and Jane are identical in interpersonal dignities and powers, in all ways except the gender pronouns that refer to them.)

PARALLELS OF WE-NESS BETWEEN DIVINE AND HUMAN

As we explore, we come upon certain Christian thoughts imputed to the mysteries of the Three. Cardinal Danielou has put it well: the three Persons of the Trinity—Father, Son, and Holy Spirit—are a WE, and also a *One*-ness, made One in their relationship-as-Three.[2] As we have said, they are engaged in the utterly complete giving and receiving of love among their Three. Their kind of giving and receiving is notably parallel to the human-human giving and receiving that we have been studying through the co-statements, though our human version of that is of course only a very faint version of the divine relationship. Because of this parallel, we can imagine that our relationships, along with our giving and receiving of meanings in this peculiar kind of love, are made in the image of the Trinity. Therefore, we can invite the Trinity and their love into our human-human relationships.

We have heard that "God is love." We can also say: "God is relational; God is WE-hood." God is beneficial, resonant, life-giving, and these functions obviously require relationality. We expect that these spiritual relationships of love cannot, by their very nature, be closed or limited or contained inside the One-ness of the Holy Three. Rather, the very nature of love is such that given-and-received love will always be magnified, and will overflow out of the Trinity and into us. "My cup runneth over!" (Ps 23:5 KJV). So it becomes available to us humans, as we allow the Trinity's love to inform our relationships with their ways of mutually loving each other. Then we may be given more ability to deepen our relationships with other humans, and also with the Trinity itself. We will explicitly invite the Holy Trinity—the Holy Spirit and the Father and the Son—into our human dialogues. Thus we hope to become more open to receive their image, their quality of loving each other,

---

2. Danielou, *God's Life*, 46.

and so make our relationships deeply divine, as well as more deeply human. How can this happen?

Relating with the Divine:

First, let us consider a relationship between one human and one divine being. Sometimes Christians relate to the loving Persons of the Trinity one at a time: sometimes to God as the loving Father, sometimes to God as the loving Christ, and sometimes to God as the comforting, uniting Holy Spirit. Each of these is a 1:1 relationship. Each of these divine beings, taken separately, is quite loving and quite worthy of faith and devotion and adoration.

There is plenty of love to go around. One Christian may speak to another about his/her 1:1 relationship with the divine: "How is your relationship with God?" Or, "Please help me with my relationship with God." But this 1:1 kind of love may sometimes seem so satisfying to one's individual self that it may seem private, so that one may fail to carry it over to his/her relationships with others. Such failure may be one reason for our apparent need to be reminded, again and again, to "love thy neighbor" as well as to "love thy God."

Our considerations of the Trinity are not intended to supplant these 1:1 relations, but rather to help us to carry the love of one or more divine beings beyond our private individualistic gratification, and into our interpersonal relations, and our missions in the world, where we recognize that our relations with everyone can indeed be in the image of the Trinity.

Going on with our guided meditation, we can say that it is quite a privilege to think of God not only as a Oneness, but also as a WE. The interaction among the unified Three is very fruitful, and their interaction itself comes to fruition as a wellspring to each of us. So we can say, "*Our* cup runneth over" (Ps 23:5 KJV, with slight paraphrase). So an individual human (say, Jane) could relate to God not merely as he is a single divine being, but also as a Trinity, *a we, a loving relationship* whose love for each other overflows toward us. Jane could deeply appreciate and adore the Trinity's "dance" of giving and receiving love with each other. Then she could let their love overflow into her own relationship with Bob. Of course, Bob could do the same thing.

As we consider such love overflowing from any deep and powerful relationship, we are drawn to think of human parents, and my story in the previous chapter, the story of Tum Tose. Parents become one in their loving relationship, and they readily give their relational love to their children. And their children readily receive the love that arises from the parents' one-ness. Such relational love can also occur between the partners in psychotherapy relationships such as we have been considering here.

The Fruitfulness of Love:

We postulate that each of the Three is quite able to love as an individual person, just as we humans speak of an individual human's love for someone. But as this Three-some comes together and they love each other in a way that brings a growing harmony of one-ness to them, through that harmony they become a One-some. Their mutuality is a field of synergetic begetting of more and more love. The love of the Three, as they have joined with each other as a Unity, is immensely fruitful, generating more and more love for each other, and also more and more love for each of us, both as individuals and as relationships. Their relationship itself is immensely fruitful. Their cups run over, and so our cups run over! The entire Christian church lives in the shareable over-flow of the love of the *Three*.

WELCOMING THE TRINITY

Part of their fruit is their actual invitation to us: that we should welcome them into our relationships. We believe that they-as-*One* are already reaching out to us; indeed, they are already present to us in their love. But by explicitly calling them in, we engage our own intention to receive their fruit, which helps us to consciously consent to and become aware of their presence and activity in our relationships, and their enrichment of positive expectations in our dialogues.

As we have seen in earlier chapters, each of our human-human relationships is also a WE: a unit, comprised of one partner and the other partner. These two are unified in the synergetic relationship-spirit between them. But it is not a unification that homogenizes; rather, it is a preservation of diversities in a grand unified harmony—a symphony of dialogue.

The Parallels Meet in Ultimate Relationship:

As we "call down" the Trinity, or "call in" the Trinity into our dialogue, and we welcome them, we see more clearly that the quality of co-dialogue relationship between humans is to some degree parallel to the quality of relationship between the Persons of the Trinity. We may have a tendency to assume, from Euclidean geometry, that two parallels never meet. But here, in a different kind of parallel, we see that our two parallels can and do meet. The WE-ness of the Trinity within itself meets the WE-ness of the human field of dialogue. They meet in that field of dialogue. This creates a much broader WE-ness, as divine meets human in what is one facet of what is called incarnation.

Thus, the ultimate relationship does not reside among the Three in the WE-ness of the Godhead. Likewise, the ultimate relationship does not reside in the two in the human dialogue's WE-ness. Rather, this ultimate relationship resides in the integration of those two realms, producing human relationships that are quickened by explicit and joyful recognition that the living, loving Trinity is meeting them, and in-dwelling their relationships. And we note also that the Trinity are enjoying their in-dwelling of us.

Parallels in Hymnody and Scripture:

This calls us to recognize a much fuller vision of the Trinity as the loving, gracious fellowship of Father, Son, and Holy Spirit. There are many parallels in hymns and liturgy that urge us to this vision. For example: "Draw us in Your Spirit's tether . . . all our meals and all our living make as sacraments of you . . ."³ Another example is this: "Come, Thou Almighty King . . . come thou incarnate Word . . . come Holy Comforter."⁴ Indeed, God as our Trinity is with us! Still another example is that jewel, noted above, with which we begin our worship services: "The grace of our Lord Jesus Christ, the love of God, and the fellowship of the Holy Spirit be with you."

WE-ness Overflows:

The Persons of the Trinity desire that their WE, their profound loving for each other, will overflow into our human WE-ness as energizing fruit. When we take in that fruit, we will be energized more deeply into our own human WE-relationships, so that these relationships become more open and loving. They become ultimate relationships. We recall that Jesus says: "We will come to him and make our home with him" (John 14:23 KJV). This statement of Jesus takes place in the context of his speaking to his disciples, so it could well be spoken in the plural, aimed at us humans: "We will come to them and make our home with them," and I would add a paraphrase: ". . . and make Our love infuse them."

The Co-statement as Fruit:

So we infer that our moments of good communication between humans can resonate with Jesus himself and his Father and their spirit, who are making their home with us. As part of that resonance, our human co-dialogue can generate interpersonal fruit, especially the co-statement. Thus, as we are following his command to love one another, we realize that engaging in co-dialogue and giving rise to a co-statement is one small way of loving one another—a way of being fruitful with one another.

---

3. *ELW*, #470.
4. *ELW*, #408.

The Three Persons Desire Their Love to be Fruitful in Us:

Jesus resonates with the Father, who will also send a "third," "another Counselor" (John 14:16 KJV). These Three engage in their own eternal interpretive relationship. In doing so, they generate the fruit of deep loving meanings. And they desire that this fruit, their relationship, their deep love-meanings, will be sent to us and will overflow into us. This is much like a pair of parents desires their love for each other to overflow onto their children! Tum Tose! So, in that overflow, each pair of humans may come to realize that, especially in their moments of deep relationship, they are *being lived* by the Trinity! The Trinity is not only *present* in our dialogue; they are actively *drawing us further* into their resonating presence, into their loving relationship. They are *living* us and sustaining us in such relationship, and making our relationships fruitful!

THE UNIQUENESS OF THE DOCTRINE OF THE TRINITY

Christian trinitarian theology is unique among religions. The doctrine of the Trinity describes the unification of the Three into One—not in "homogenization" of their diversities, but in "harmonization" of them. Some religions do claim a three-some in their godhead. But none to my knowledge requires the mystery that the Three-some be also unified into a One-some. This unification might look like a "constraint" on their Three-ness. But actually it functions to produce revelations about love's synergy in relational interaction, and about the nature of relationship as a love-dynamo, a synergy that *grows in relationship*. Welcoming this Three-in-One's love into our two-some co-dialogue allows us to use these revelations to enhance our own becoming harmonized and thus unified into "two-in-one." Thus we parallel the Trinity! We can even assert, as above, that the "two-in-one" in co-dialogue are accompanied by a third, a Spirit who empowers the two by unifying them.

Glimpses Into the Mystery:

The doctrine of the Trinity, and the relationships imputed to the It/Them, carry great mystery, just as every relationship carries great mystery. But maybe we can get a glimpse into the mystery by comparing certain experiences and meanings that humans may have. So we continue with our guided meditation.

First, as we have seen, the human co-statements have meanings that *endure independently* of their origins. These meanings can be appreciated by a person who had nothing to do with their moment of origin. Similarly, some scriptural words and phrases have meanings that endure. They can be appreciated independently of their historical origin. Familiar examples include these:

1. "A remnant shall return" (Isa 10:21 RSV);
2. "I am God, and not man" (Hos 11:3 KJV);
3. "Love your enemies" (Matt 5:44 KJV);
4. "Judge not that ye be not judged" (Matt 7:1 KJV);
5. "Blessed are they that mourn" (Matt 5:4 KJV);
6. "Blessed are the peacemakers" (Matt 5:9 KJV);
7. "Casting down their golden crowns around the glassy sea."[5]

The second glimpse has to do with being fully present. As a therapist, I want to be fully present to my patients. This must mean being coherent inside my "self," and thus echoing Carl Rogers. But it must mean much more than that. I, in my internally coherent self, will speak. That is, I will externalize my coherent self into words. They are *my* words, and they become part of my "larger" self. And when my internal presence is unified with my externalized words (and actions) in this way, we may say that I am in full presence. In complex system theory, we may say that "I" and "my words and behaviors" are both entities that maintain their discreet identity while also they combine into a unity.

This unifying of a self plus his/her words offers us a parallel with the unifying of the Father and his Word into One. Recall that, according to Christian theology, the Father's Son is also his Word. This gives us a glimpse of what it may mean that they are in

---

5. *ELW*, #413.

unification. If I can be one with my words, then I get a glimpse of what it might mean that God the Father is one with his Word. "In the beginning was the Word, and the Word was with God and the Word was God" (John 1:1 KJV).

A third glimpse occurs when we notice that our human love is not a one-way thing. When I love my patient or my friend in this "dialogue" way, it is likely that my love will evoke loving responses from him/her. We will have a "charmed loop," where each cycle of loving and responding will spontaneously evoke more love for each partner. In this charmed loop, there will also spontaneously come to be more love to give to others outside our dialogue. And this fruitful process is parallel to what we have already attributed to the powerhouse generator of love that is the Trinity.

God's Transactions with Us, and Our Readiness:

The mystery includes God's many transactions with us: both giving to us and receiving from us. Let us focus on some of the contents of these transactions. First, we turn to God's action. It is he who offers to come to us. He proffers divine gifts of love and communion. As he gives, we receive. His gifts will affect many aspects of our co-dialogue. "Calling in the Trinity" is a transactional step. Our "calling in" indicates our readiness to recognize the Trinity's coming *into* us, into our relationships, from outside us. In our response to such a gift, God receives our praise and prayer and offerings.

We speak of the individual Persons of the Trinity, as well as the "whole" Trinity. None of these considerations should be taken to suggest any limitation in devotion to any one Person of the Trinity. We speak of the different Persons at the risk of reification; we do so partly in order to preserve the connection with salvation history: The Father in creation, the Son in incarnation, the Holy Spirit acting especially at Pentecost and far beyond. As we receive the Three Persons in their Tri-Unity, we hope that their togetherness—their ability to be united in togetherness—will be for us a source of inspiration for our relationships.

Magnifying *Being*, Both Divine and Human:

The mystery continues further, as each Person of the Trinity is magnified in his being by sharing his joy and synergy with the other two. Imagine the weal and joy and synergy and creativity of the fellowship-relationship of the Three Persons. Each of them receives his *being*, magnifies his *being*, is magnified in his *being*, by his joy and synergy with the others! And in parallel, we notice that for us humans in co-dialogue, we too experience our own being as magnified *because* we develop relationships in which our partner's being is magnified.

THE GREAT BENEDICTION AND MY TEPID ATTENTION

The benediction at the head of this chapter is a magnificent gift from God. "The grace of our Lord Jesus Christ, the love of God, and the fellowship of the Holy Spirit be with you all." For many years, I heard this benediction, from 2 Corinthians, and received it as a merely beautiful but impotent set of words. Perhaps you, too, have noticed how such words often recede into powerlessness. Only after years of studying relationships, both human and divine, did I "wake up" and begin to hear it, and let it perform its meaning upon me. It is a performative, and a very rich blessing. It really does "perform" the act of "calling in" the full relationship itself: the Son, the Father, and the Holy Spirit of fellowship.

But I also had assumed that it was addressed to us as individuals. Looking closer, we can see that this profound combination—grace and love and fellowship—not only fills us as individuals, and fills our community the church, but also fills our dialogue relationships. It is as if each partner offers this benediction to his/her dialogue partner continually. Thus, we are again given an ideal of what can happen between one human and another. Also, let us allow that spirit of communion to enter us so much that we become able to offer the same blessing to any and all persons.

Offering Presence and Relationship:

Especially in the context of our receiving this powerful trinitarian benediction, we may co-create new relational meanings, which can bear fruit in the occurrence of a co-statement. This co-statement may even heal certain differences between the partners, as described in chapter one. As we are moved to take on this ideal, these gifts from the Trinity support and further our fellowship-in-spirit, our gracious and loving relations with one another, our co-creatings with one another. Indeed, these gifts of their presence generate presence in us. And our "being present" will also bring us closer to fulfilling Jesus' commandment: "... love one another, as I have loved you" (John 15:12 KJV). The way in which he loved us is through his presence-in-relationship, through his presenting himself to us as the One who somehow also carries the Father and the Holy Spirit. In that, we ourselves become equipped to offer presence, to present and invite *relational presence* with all we meet.

CHAPLAIN TRAINEES ASK QUESTIONS

As I was discussing these co-statements with some chaplain trainees, one of them asked me whether such wonderful co-creations might happen not only between two humans, but also in the relationship between a human and God. So I started looking into my prayer journal, and inviting others to look into theirs. I discovered that some of my statements had more meaning and power and even "being"—suggesting a role of God in their creation. Does this suggest WE-hood between me and God? And also, of course, between you and God.

Then the question of Spirit arose. Can these co-creatings be actual evidence of the working of spirit? It is said by Buber: "When you and I talk, there is spirit. It is not that spirit is *in* you, or *in* me; rather, spirit is between us." This leads me to the notion that our co-dialogues and co-creations are generated in spirit.

But as Christians, the chaplains wanted to know whether that spirit is indeed the Holy Spirit of Christ. Could the Holy Spirit partake in an activity such as that? We turn to the Nicene Creed, the version that has been used in Western Christianity since the sixth or seventh century CE.[6] There we find that the Holy Spirit "proceedeth from the Father and the Son. And together with the Father and the Son, he is worshiped and glorified."

"Proceedeth" From the Relationship Between the Father and the Son:

Never shy to speculate, I wondered whether this might mean that the Holy Spirit "proceedeth" from the relationship, the verbal interactions between the Father and the Son. If so, then the Holy Spirit is himself co-created from the Father and the Son! (The inversion of this—that the Son himself is co-created from the Father and the Spirit—in mutual co-creation—is probably also valid in "divine mechanics" such as we are considering, but it cannot be elaborated here.)

Having proceeded from their relationship, having been given *being* from their relationship, the Holy Spirit feeds back into their charmed loop and connects them as they all Three give and receive with each other. And the Holy Spirit takes up his own *being*, and proceeds to go out and be active in the world, to love us and comfort us and bless us by connecting us with each other and also with him/them.

TURNING TO DEVOTIONAL LIFE WITH THE TRINITY

Then the dance begins to grow even larger. The parallels meet. We see the cross-fertilizations between the two realms. The divine "*relationships-with-co-creating*," the Father and the Son and the Holy Spirit, co-create the fruit of their love for us. And we see the human-human "*relationships-with-co-creating*," as the partners co-create their fruit, which is verbal love. These are new meanings, "contagious" meanings, which can be enjoyed and used by others. Such co-creating of new meaning occurs in both realms. The

---

6. Darrell Jodock, personal communication.

"what" that is co-created in the divine process seems quite different from the "what" of human-human co-creations. But the process of co-creating those divine "whats" is similar in form to the process of the "whats" that occur between persons.

Our devotional life is surely a cross-fertilization of both kinds of "whats." So let us shift from purely dialogical considerations of the Trinity, toward their presence with us in every moment. Let us turn more to Scripture and theology, and to our devotional life.

In earlier chapters, I have given a few examples of co-created statements in human-human co-dialogue. In contrast, here are a few examples of verbal interaction, divine conversation, between the Father and his incarnated Son.

1. "Thou art my beloved Son, in whom I am well pleased" (Mark 1:11 KJV). Jesus responded to this supreme affirmation by going into temptation, where he called on the word of his Father. "It is written, 'Man shall not live by bread alone, but by every word that proceedeth out of the mouth of God'" (Matt 4:4 KJV).
2. "The Lord said to my Lord, Sit thou on my right hand, till I make thine enemies thy footstool" (Mark 12:36 KJV).
3. "And the glory which Thou gavest me I have given them; that they may be one even as we are one" (John 17:22 KJV).
4. ". . . that the love with which thou hast loved me may be in them, and I in them" (John 17:26 RSV).
5. "My God, my God, why hast Thou forsaken me?" (Mark 15:34 KJV). This rupture of their relationship (or at least of Jesus's awareness of their relationship) was answered by God the Father only in the resurrection of Jesus as the Christ.

Our God has taken the initiative, and has come at us with Incarnation. "And the Word was made flesh and dwelt among us" (John 1:14 KJV). Contemplating that glory offers a treasury of images of these cross-overs between divine and human. One example of such a cross-over occurs in music. We in our human-human relationships can access new levels of grace and love and communion. One example occurs when we sing together the great old hymn,

"When in our music God is glorified."[7] It goes on to say: "How often making music we have found a new dimension in the world of sound!" Indeed, how often making worship we have found a new dimension, ever new, as the Incarnation lights up for us once again.

In this Incarnation, we learn again that the Trinity desires to join us. The Spirit "intercedes for us with sighs too deep for words" (Rom 8:26 RSV); the Jesus of the Gospels teaches us, and will go and build mansions for us (John 14:2, my paraphrase); the Holy Spirit is guiding and uniting us; the resurrected Christ "liveth to make intercession" (Heb 7:25 KJV) for them.

We note that each of these three Persons has a fundamental nature that is radically different from that of the other Two. For this reason, we can expect that their interaction of differentnesses, their relationship *in* their diversity, is even more powerful in fruitfulness. Their love (in their unified Oneness) super-saturates us in our relationships. The Trinity are *present* with us, and their wholeness seeks to include all of us, drawing us into greater and greater wholeness and integration with the whole world. We are joined to a community of love, in the household of love. We may take the epigram of this chapter to mean that individually and also in all our relationships, the Trinity is present, waiting to be recognized more and more fully as *the power of loving unification*, and to join with us more and more fully. This power connects us, unifies all of us with itself, and with each other in our joys and our sorrows.

The Trinity thus quickens all our relationships, our actions, our interpersonal conversations. By the Trinity's joining with us, bringing divine levels of hope and grace and love and communion, we are made able to appropriate, to enliven, to put into daily co-dialogue the trinitarian words of our Scriptures and worship. Our liturgy includes so many references to the Trinity, such as the examples above. We call on the Trinity in so many ways—yet we can go so much further in recognizing the Trinity's role in our dialogues and our daily lives.

---

7. *ELW*, #850.

Perfectly Natural and Perfectly Supernatural: An Indwelling Companion:

As I write this, I hope that it will be perfectly natural (and perfectly supernatural) for you and me to know the Holy Trinity as a constantly in-dwelling companion, especially as we contemplate what happens in our best relationships, and with our dialogue partners. We are envisioning that our dialogue relationships are made in the image of God the Trinity! This Trinity gives theirself to us, and we recognize The Trinity as already present in our relationships, even as they grace our own openness to receive them. We consent with our will to this in-dwelling of the Trinity. We may then be led to find ways to make all our relationships better.

Openness:

One way of doing that is to become more aware of the openness of the Persons of the Trinity with each other—utterly complete openness—and to receive that openness as an ideal for our selves and our relationships. (Such openness does not mean that we can feel free to say anything that comes into our mind regardless of our connection with the patient; rather, it suggests a kind of interpersonal linking that opens us to receive whatever arises in our soul-contact with the patient.)

Perfectly Super-natural: The Mystery of Not Knowing:

Because of the consummate mystery of every relationship and every awareness, our resonating awarenesses mean that we will receive the Trinity even in ways that we may not recognize. That is, we may join the patriarch Jacob in his dream, when he said: "Surely the Lord is in this place, and I knew it not" (Gen 28:16 KJV). Such manifestations of mystery may be experienced as super-natural. We may receive their supernatural joining with us in the mystery of our relationships, and perhaps not realize it.

BEING LED INTO JESUS'S GREAT COMMANDMENT

But we will be led anyway, in mystery, ineffably, into further giving and receiving loving presence and personhood with each other. In so doing, we will come to know—and fulfill—Jesus's great commandment, as we noted above: "Love one another, as I have loved you" (John 15:12 KJV).

This great commandment has many possible interpretations. One of them that I particularly like is this: "Give your presence and personhood to one another, in your verbal interactions, as I have given my presence and personhood to you in our verbal interactions." And we recall that Jesus's presence includes his lively relationship with his Father: "He who has seen me has seen the Father" (John 14:9 KJV).

Jesus famously said: "If two of you agree on earth about anything they ask, it will be done for them by my Father in heaven. For where two or three are gathered in My name, there am I in the midst of them" (Matt 18:20 RSV). That is as if he says: "My presence is in the midst of them." Here we see the involvement of the Father in Jesus's presence. Also we understand that the Holy Spirit is present in such an occasion, especially for us today, so long after the human Jesus became the resurrected Christ. It is as if Jesus said: "Not only am I there in the midst of those humans, but also My Father and My Spirit are there in the midst of them, unifying them and in-dwelling them."

Another interpretation suggests that he loved them by humbling himself and washing their feet (John 13:14 KJV, my paraphrase). But for us today, we feel little need to have our feet washed. We understand "humbling" in other ways. This may mean to "wash" the burdens from one another *during our co-dialogues*. That is, we may *give unburdening to an other, and let ourself receive unburdening from an other.* Paul says, in Gal 6:2 (RSV) "Bear one another's burdens and so fulfill the law of Christ." And we do so in joy. And thereby we become unified with each other and with the Trinity's joy.

TRANSCENDING WORDS

In this work, we have started our considerations with human verbal interactions which occur in a field of dialogue. We have focused on the words that are given and received. Our dialogues, and also our prayer and worship, are largely verbal rhetorical systems. But we also want to remain aware of many Christian actions that transcend words: baptism, laying on of hands, washing feet, some forms of prayer, healing, participating in Eucharist. These are also ways of "communicating," of affecting one another, beyond words. Yet for now we must limit ourselves to the verbal, and we claim the miracle that the full Trinity is present with us *in our verbal relationships!* And as yet another miracle, this presence of the Trinity will often be magnified in us as we practice it.

SO WHAT? WHAT DIFFERENCE DOES IT MAKE?

Now we will be presumptuous, and ask: "OK. So what? We are gathered in Jesus's name. He and his Father and their Spirit are present in our gathering. What difference does that make in what we are exchanging with each other? Does our belief in their presence really produce any deeper awarenesses and fruit in our exchanges?" Surely we would like to answer "yes" to that.

The answer includes our realizing that we will be taken further in our ideal of open sharing, our mutual affirmation and mutual unburdening. We receive our awarenesses of their presence and their effect upon us—their inspiration upon us—in every particular gathering. And their effect may lead us more often into co-dialogue, and may even produce moments of coming together in the mutuality of co-statements.

Further, in following him, in his name, when I reach out to some other human in loving relationship, I will join this dance of God's Incarnation and thus of God's Trinity. In the Incarnation, Jesus came to be present with us: not merely seeing us from the outside, as in judgment; but being *with* us from the inside, in compassion. Thus, he commits an act of knowing us, not through objective observation, not through seeing us from outside, but through the coalescence of his and our insides!

The parallel is this. For me as a therapist, I surrender any urge to know the person by observing him/her from outside, perhaps even without his/her consent. I try to know that person not only with their consent, but with their active co-operation—from inside their self! Then I become aware that there is a "vehicle" that goes from my insideness into the field of interaction between us, and then into the other's insideness. That vehicle is language, words: my words and patients' words and, of course, the Word.

What Can I Give to Relationship?:

Putting together several theological pieces, we can say that God gave his *Word*, who is his only begotten Son, to be in relationship with us, and to be in dialogue with us. In a pale but definite similarity, I can give my words to a patient. But I do this best when I am led by God The Trinity. To follow The Trinity means (among other things) to proclaim the good news, using words! I will give what I can from my heart. How do I do that? My chief answer is that I will pray to take on the Trinity. I will let that benediction be performed upon me—the grace, love, and communion—and these three gifts will make "me" unified with my words and actions, and with the needs of my dialogue partners. I will offer a context that is as free as possible from my own *individual* thoughts and needs and expectations, so as to hear and receive the partner's thoughts and needs and expectations—and to respond soulfully in relational words from my own insides, as inspired by the Trinity.

A VAST TREASURE-HOUSE

In doing such things, we occupy a vast splendid treasure-house of relationships in Godhead. When we gather in this Name, we are given the incredible privilege of handling the "crown jewels" of the Trinity, far, far more splendid than the crown jewels of England or Iran. And they are ours. They are for each of us to hold and grow from. We bask in the Trinity of Father, Son, Holy Spirit: the grace of our Lord Jesus Christ, the love of the Father, and the fellowship of the Holy Spirit. We pray to the Father, through the Son, in the Holy Spirit! We pray for the power to call in the immense soul-enlivening beauty of such holiness. We invite each other to partake of this great treasure-feast, and we dance in it together. In so doing we encounter the Holy Community. We are invited to be newly drawn into his/their presence, and into relations with those who are already aware of receiving his love. We recall again the old hymn: "Draw us in the Spirit's tether . . ."[8]

The Encounter with Otherness: Human and Divine:

Let us close this work with a quote from Johnson, about the Holy Community. "Christianity was from the beginning an intensely social religion, in which the encounter with the otherness of the divine, of God, is found in encounter with the otherness of other people."[9]

And magnificently, the prototype and template of that encounter with otherness was already the Christian Trinity as it/they indwelled those early believers and also indwelled their relationships. Now the Trinity's Three continue to indwell and magnify all our relational love. So we accept the invitation to explore and resonate with this abundance of love and relationship and Spirit, in these divine human relationships. Hallelujah!

---

8. *ELW*, #470.
9. Johnson, *Early Christianity*, lecture 19.

Glossary

with concept clarifications

Charmed feedback loop: This is the opposite of a "vicious cycle" in which things get worse and worse as the system functions. In co-dialogue (see "Co-dialogue" below) and in any charmed loop, things get better and better as the system functions.

Context: See "Element and context" below.

Co-created: Since we are concerned with two partners in dialogue, we want to notice how well they function together to produce new meanings. When it is clear that a particular new meaning has emerged from the participation of both partners, we say that the new meaning is co-created. See "Co-statement."

Co-dialogue: Many writings that are labeled "dialogue" consist of questions directed to some prominent person by an interviewer, whose role is to evoke new meanings from the prominent person, but not to contribute to them. Here, we are dealing with a different kind of dialogue in which one partner's contributions are just as important as the other partner's. Each partner evokes new meanings from the other partner and also allows him/herself to be affected by those new meanings. So we say that their meanings are co-created, and thus that they are in co-dialogue.

Glossary

Co-statement: Occasionally, there is a statement that clearly contains within itself references to contributions by both partners. This kind of statement occurs in a field of co-dialogue, is thus said to be co-created, and we can call it a co-statement.

Dialogue: Here we use this word to apply to a verbal interchange of statements between only two partners, who are affecting each other with new meanings about each other. Most of the new meanings are rather prosaic, and produce little change in the subsequent flow of meanings. But occasionally, a statement is noticed to be followed by large, important increases in the meanings and topics available for discussion. Each such statement thus functions as a context (see entry above) for integrating more and more meanings. We say that it has enlarged the meaning-flow.

Economy, old/new: An ordinary economy is generally assumed to be a zero-sum process. If I give you some of my water, you will have more water, but I will have less. But in many spiritual transactions, the reverse is true. There is a new economy. Personhood is a quality that has the property of blessing both partners. In giving you a spiritual gift, such as personhood, you will have more of it, but I also will have more of it. We can call this a "charmed feedback loop" (see entry above). See "Personhood."

Element and context: For us, these two are distinguished by their effects on the meaning-flow of the subsequent dialogue. Every statement begins its life in the field as an element, which may be nothing more than a carrier of information. It may have very little effect on the meaning-flow. But some statements are surprising, and these produce great broadening of the topics in the meaning-flow. Thus we say that they function as contexts, integrating the new topics. For example, refer to Carol's repeated use of the phrase "dried up and cut off," and my eventual "hearing" it in the new context of the story of the dry bones.

GLOSSARY

Field: The two partners plus all of their statements to each other plus the meanings and their flow, constitute the field of dialogue. The field holds statements, and carries them between the partners. Any statement can be extracted from the field and examined as a free-standing entity. This simple fact proves the existence of the field as a third entity in the dialogue, since there is no other "place" from which the statement can be extracted.

Grace: We sometimes speak of a field of grace. This refers to interactions that, without recognizable effort, produce desirable results for both partners. These results occur not so much because they were desired or striven for, but because of the freedom of spontaneous expression. Unexpected new blessed meaning can emerge: unbidden, surprising, refreshing, gratifying.

Information: This can be briefly defined as news of difference. When it is spoken, it becomes an element in the dialogue.

Invert: In a dialogue, the most obvious example of inverting occurs when a partner who is in the role of "speaker" comes to the end of one episode of speaking, and he/she then becomes silent and "inverts" to taking the role of listener. Another dimension of inverting can be seen when the effect of a statement on the meaning-flow of the dialogue changes (inverts) from that of "element bearing news of difference" to that of context (see "Context" above).

It/Them: This awkward form refers to the Trinity in a way that is intended to preserve awareness that the Trinity is at once a "One," and simultaneously a "Three." Usually, I will use the plural form "them" for ease of readability.

Meaning-flow: As the dialogue proceeds, the meaning of one statement (by either partner) affects the flow of meanings into the future dialogue, as they give and receive meanings with each other. This effect can be small or large. Especially if the statement has a new and surprising nature, it can produce major broadening of the topics in the meaning-flow. A major effect on meaning-flow is one result of the speaking of a co-statement.

Mutuality: A quality of relationship in dialogue in which meanings are co-created in a way that is beneficial to both partners. This quality could give rise to the paraphrase of Carol's co-statement which is found in the text: "Now I can see that I am not, after all, a person who cannot be affected by some positive message. And I see that you can see that too." It could also give rise to another paraphrase: "I am loved not just by you, but also by noticing myself-responding-to-your-love." Mutuality is closely related to love. It is a field of synergetic begetting of more and more communicated love.

Personhood: A person is a living being who has awarenesses of identity and love and will, and also is willing and able to give and receive these with other persons. He/she assumes that these others have similar awarenesses, and abilities to communicate them. Personhood is the state of having and using these gifts. For example, imagine that one partner speaks a co-statement, and does so in a way that combines his/her own internal awarenesses with external awarenesses of his partner. Then we can say that he/she is enjoying personhood. One person's expression of his/her personhood may evoke similar expressions of personhood from his/her dialogue partner. When personhood is mutually exchanged in this way, we can see evidence of the new economy (see "Economy, old/new" above).

Self: I use this term by itself rather than in the conventional forms such as "himself" or "herself," in order to emphasize that the self can be taken conceptually as a separate entity, and that certain considerations are clearer with that usage. (The self is of course simultaneously separate and also in relationship.)

Soul-speak: This designation is somewhat broader but also less powerful than personhood. Sometimes one partner speaks a statement that can be clearly recognized as coming from deep inside him/her. It finds resonance within the listener. It is thus a very valuable contribution to the dialogue. It is a sharing of self. But it fails to be a co-statement in that it does not contain reference to contributions of the other partner. Nevertheless, it is aimed at the partner, and appreciated by the partner.

Statement: any verbal production (one statement or several statements) that occurs between the partners in a dialogue. This includes interrogative statements. Every statement has some effect on the flow of meaning after it is spoken. When we monitor the meaning-flow, we find that most statements have little effect, but some have very large effects. A co-statement is the best example of a statement that has very large effects. It becomes a context for gathering and integrating many new meanings and also much mutuality.

Bibliography

Anderson, Harlene. "Listening, Hearing and Speaking: Brief Thoughts on the Relationship to Dialogue." *Psychological Opinions*, Spring 2016. https://www.taosinstitute.net/files/Content/5692909/Listen,_Hear_and_Speak_for_Opinions_-_Anderson,_H..pdf.
Bertalanffy, Ludwig von. *General Systems Theory*. New York: Braziller, 1969.
Buber, Martin. *I and Thou*. Translated by Ronald Gregor Smith. New York: Scribner's, 1958.
———. *Tales of the Hasidim: The Early Masters*. New York: Schocken, 1947.
Danielou, Jean. *God's Life in Us*. Wilkes-Barre, PA: Dimension, 1969.
De Chardin, Pierre Teilhard. *The Phenomenon of Man*. Translated by Bernard Wall. New York: Harper & Row, 1959.
De Quincey, Christian. *Radical Knowing: Understanding Consciousness through Relationship*. Rochester, VT: Park Street, 2005.
Dostoyevsky, Fyodor. *The Brothers Karamazov*. San Francisco: North Point, 1990.
Erikson, Erik H. *Childhood and Society*. New York: Norton, 1963.
Evangelical Lutheran Church in America. *Evangelical Lutheran Worship (ELW)*. Minneapolis: Fortress, 2006.
Greening, Tom. Former editor of the Journal of Humanistic Psychology.
Gunter, Richard. *Sentences in Dialogue*. Columbia, SC: Hornbeam, 1974.
Johnson, Luke. *Early Christianity: The Experience of the Divine*. The Great Courses. CD-ROM. Chantilly, VA: The Teaching Company, 2013.
Kaufman, Gershon. *Shame: The Power of Caring*. New York: Schenkman, 1983.
Mesle, C. Robert. "Aesthetic Value and Relational Power: An Essay on Personhood." *Process Studies* 13, no. 1 (Spring 1983) 59–70. http://www.religion-online.org/article/aesthetic-value-and-relational-power-an-essay-on-personhood/.
Nouwen, Henri. *The Wounded Healer*. New York: Image, 1972.
O'Donnell, John, SJ. *Hans Urs von Balthasar*. Outstanding Christian Thinkers. Collegeville, MN: Liturgical, 1992.

Reeves, Ralph. "The Co-Statement: Objective Evidence for a Science of Subjectivity." *Journal of Humanistic Psychology* 46, no. 2 (April 2006) 209–33.

Schut, Michael, ed. *Simpler Living, Compassionate Life: A Christian Perspective*. New York: Morehouse, 1999.

www.ingramcontent.com/pod-product-compliance
Lightning Source LLC
Chambersburg PA
CBHW070256100426
42743CB00011B/2248